THE SOUL BONDAGE

THE HOUSE OF ISRAEL OHIO

SOUL BONDAGE
DISCOVERING TRUE DELIVERANCE

GERALD "HOSHEA" WILLIAMS JR.

Copyright © 2019 by Gerald "Hoshea" Williams Jr.

Publishing Services by Happy Self Publishing
www.happyselfpublishing.com

Year: 2019

All rights reserved. No part of this book may be reproduced or transmitted in any form or by any means without written permission from the author.

Printed in USA by ..

ACKNOWLEDGMENTS

This book has been a long process of development and patience. With the deepest sense of gratitude, I, Gerald "Hoshea" Williams Jr. would like to say thank you to:

i. The House of Israel Ohio[1] Team class of 2014-2016 and the class of 2018-2019. You have influenced, cultivated, and helped the core understanding of Soul Bondage come to be.

ii. Derek Echad Israelite Beit Midrash (One Way Israelite House of Study)[2]. Thank you for being a mentor, investigator, corrector, brother, and friend, Moreh Tony "AdoniYah" Lewis. Even when we do not agree, we continue in our bond.

---

[1] http://houseofisraelohio.com
[2] https://derekechad.com

iii. Amana BaYah[3], without your diligent, detailed note taking of the classes in the season of 2016, I would not have had the idea to create this.
iv. My daughter Mia, whose courage has been an example for me to model in those seasons of adversities. When others would quit, I thank you for not quitting on me or yourself. You have true grit.

---

[3] http://amanabayah.com

TABLE OF CONTENTS

Acknowledgments 5

One: Soul Bondage Illustration 9

Two: Let Us Explain 13
    A Hebrew Perspective 14
    My Personal Soul Bondage: 18

Three: Soul Mastery Not Soul Ties 21

Four: Slaves to Infirmity 35
    Infirmity Caused by Emotional and Spiritual Conflict 47

Five: Defining a Soul 59
    The Intangible Soul 65
    Tangible Effects on the Intangible Soul 69

Six: The Recompense Due 73
    What is Recompense? 74
    The Offended Soul 76
    A Remedy for the Offended Soul 85
    A Soul that is Stained 93

Seven: The Legalities of Soul Bondage 99
    Christ Ordained Authority 104
    Torah Ordained Authority 107
    Numbers 30 Breakdown 109
    Order of the Husband and Wife 120
    How Do I Know If I Have Authority (woman)? . 122
    What Happened to My Authority (man)? 125
    Temperance 129
    The Disowned Child 130

Eight: From Infirmity to Freedom 135
    The Anointing Destroys the Yoke. 136

About Hoshea 141
    The Call: 142
    Accomplishments: 143
    Areas of Study: 143
    My Personal Soul Bondage: 144

References 145

One

SOUL BONDAGE ILLUSTRATION

Figure 1 - Original considered cover art

Who is this man with his finger to his lips? The image of a young man chained in a dark, solemn place, with cold, empty walls, illustrates the conflict of the dark force over him. The not so obvious message is the choice of colors used in the design. Our young captor in an all-red color grade represents the bound soul. With the color contrast of black and white next to the red, hopefully, it makes someone think; the man with the finger possibly isn't even there.

Maybe the chains, the walls, and the bondage aren't really happening in a physical realm. A young man has been brought into captivity, forced into silence, trapped on a plane where only the bound soul can recognize.

Walter A. Constant masterfully captures the soul of a man being bound by this entity demanding silence and submission. The hopelessness in the eyes of the bound soul reminds us of the scripture in Isaiah 61:1:

> *The Spirit of the Lord GOD is upon me; because the LORD hath anointed me to preach good tidings unto the meek; he hath sent me to bind up the brokenhearted, to proclaim liberty to the captives, and the opening of the prison to them that are bound;*
> *-King James Version.*

Can you identify with the feeling of being bound in an area of your life? Whether it is spiritual, physical, mental or financial? Hopefully, when you have made it to the end of this book you can see where to apply change. Changes once implemented that bring about a liberty and newness of life. A revelation that sparks a desire to seek and search for more understanding. An inspiration that awakens a sleeping gift or call that has been on the shelf too long.

Two

LET US EXPLAIN

What you are about to read was forged through adversity and pain. What was supposed to be a simple assembling of notes turned into a three-year process. Starting in the summer of 2016, two major transitions delayed its completion until now.

The House of Israel Ohio is a small body of believers in the Messiah who meet to study the Torah[4] and New Testament writings. Each Sabbath, they investigate how the scriptures and His spirit is guiding them to be more effective in His Kingdom.

During the Passover season of 2016, *The House of Israel Ohio* was faced with a challenge. The challenge was to let Israel know to look beyond just

---

[4] "Torah" –Teaching and instructions of the Most High God, the five books of Moses, often mistranslated as law, #H8451 & #H3384

the memorial of their freedom from Egypt at Passover. It was time to also work at being free in the soul. Whether, this was the local community of Israel at *The House of Israel Ohio* or the diaspora, the challenge was set.

There is more to our soul bondage than what most people have learned from the Christian movement and we at *The House of Israel Ohio* were ready to investigate. Our studying began, and revelations came, we knew the information we were uncovering needed to be published for the nations. The format of a book came only when Amana BaYah shared with us all the notes she had taken from the lessons and discussions we had in class. Seeing the volume of information written out became an inspiration to put in a book format. I, Hoshea, have taken the liberty to assemble the notes, revelations, conversations, lessons, and new insight into what we learned.

Hopefully, in the process of reading, you will be able to discern the areas in your life, your family's and friends' lives, where bondages of the soul have kept them bound.

A Hebrew Perspective

This would be a good book for you if you:
  i. Have a relationship with the Messiah
  ii. Have been struggling with the roller coaster of sin

iii. Are not familiar with the law and what role it plays in spiritual warfare
iv. Are familiar with the Torah and are looking for some of the spiritual applications of the law
v. Have a call on your life for deliverance
vi. Struggle with abusive relationships and substance abuse
vii. Are a leader over a group that is interested in dissecting scriptures. This book offers a lot of hidden gems.

At the bottom of each page, when necessary, I took the liberty to add reference notes pointing to another translation or pronunciation of the word. These notes may also offer commentary when necessary for clarity. The research references are also placed here in the footer, usually indicated by a small number next to the word. A glossary of words used is in the rear of the book, which may also be helpful.

As a Hebrew believer in the Messiah, I will be using the natural principles governing the earth called the Torah. This helps establish a basis for the spiritual principles we, at times, are so blindly unaware of. When the common Church chose to leave the Torah, the law, and its judgments, it caused blindness. Blindness to so many potential natural consequences the natural law brings as results to our actions outside of His will.

Y'shua[5] and Paul both make a simple account in scriptures of how our inability to discern the "earthly/natural things" of Elohim[6], *first,* makes it difficult for us to understand the spiritual principles. Scriptures like John 3:12 and I Corinthians 15:46 reads:

> *If I told you earthly things and you don't believe, how will you believe if I tell you heavenly things?*
> *John 3:12*
>
> *However that which is spiritual isn't first, but that which is natural, then that which is spiritual.*
> *1 Corinthians 15:46 (WEB)*

My goal is to offer these natural/earthly principles according to the Torah and to show the associated spiritual principles. This will give you the ability to fight *the Adversary*[7] on terms and grounds he must legally abide by. Many of us have tried to operate or understand the supernatural while not recognizing the 'natural' before the 'super' is added.

---

[5] "Y'shua" – Name of the Messiah in the NT meaning "Salvation". Often translated as Jesus, Yeshua, Yahshua, Yahawashi even Yehoshua.
[6] "Elohim" – Literally meaning Mighty One or Powers whether the supreme power or celestial powers.
[7] "HaSatan" – the adversary - often translated as Satan

A Hebraic method of study commonly used to exegesis[8] scriptures is called "PaRDeS."[9] This is the method of interpretation I will be using throughout the book. PaRDeS is an acronym meaning:

i. **P**eshat- a simple rational interpretation
ii. **R**emez- inference a meaning beyond just the literal sense. Usually found by referring back to previous text.
iii. **D**rash- to seek out, study or to inquire. Usually through discussion called "MiDrash."
iv. **S**od - mysteries within the text given by revelation or inspiration. Please allow the Spirit to offer this to you at what level He chooses. There will be no mystical interpretations offered.

PaRDeS isn't always plainly seen, so I took the liberty to draw it out occasionally, to help develop a sensitivity to the style.

Here is another set of hermeneutic rules used for biblical interpretation I also applied:

> Principle #1: The scriptures cannot contradict.
> Principle #2: Keep the text in context.

---

[8] Exegesis - critical explanation or interpretation of a text or portion of a text, especially of the Bible.
[9] The Jewish Encyclopedia, NY.: Funk & Wagnalls Co., 1906,

Principle #3: Consider the greater principle of what is being said. This is called Kal V'chomer, meaning light and heavy or the weightier matter.

These do work in sequence, so if the understanding is not found from following the first principle, then we move to the next principle and so on.

My Personal Soul Bondage:

Starting in the fourth grade, I was exposed to voyeurism on a regular basis. By the time I was in the seventh grade, I had a hardcore porn collection of five movies. My wife tells me how she was never even exposed to pornography till I brought it around before we got married and then into the marriage. Ministering with the monkey of lust on my back made me begin to search. The infirmity in my walk that I experienced was not only frustrating but embarrassing. I recognized there was something missing in my walk with the Messiah, so everyone told me I needed the Spirit. I received the Spirit, then I was told I needed to get the fire of the spirit, the worship of the spirit, the joy of the spirit, the power of the spirit, and so I became a prayer warrior.

So many answers, but I was never offered principles that caused me to take ownership of my iniquity and speak out against the corruption in my soul. This has caused me to have a heart for those in the broken system of medicating problems and not getting to the root cause. The principles that I speak of are from the law, and most evangelicals are so scared of falling into the bondage of legalism that they would rather stay bound to sin.

If you have been a victim of emotionalism offered as spiritualism and answers offered as solutions, then you need to keep reading. The principles that you are going to read about will give the edge over addictions, bondages, and traps that have kept you or someone that you love bound. To find out more about my testimony and journey, please visit the *About Hoshea* section in the rear of the book.

Three

SOUL MASTERY NOT SOUL TIES

The first thing I want to establish is not associating the Christian concept of *soul ties* with the Hebraic concept of soul bondage. In this first section, I will begin by training for some and re-training for others on the thought process for reflecting a master-slave relationship versus a *soul tie*.

The best way to describe a soul tie, in its simplest definition, is *an intense, intimate, or very close relationship or friendship.* [10] Soul ties are often spoken of in the Christian charismatic or demonic

---

[10] For more information about soul ties ref.: ISBN-10: 0892280166 – "Soul Ties" by: Frank Hammond

deliverance type of ministries. Soul ties are spoken of with a negative connotation, almost like soul ties are a sin[11]. The scriptures do not show us a model saying; *you are corrupt and defiled if you care intensely for someone.* This is a general concept of *soul ties,* but we will dig more in-depth into this view later.

When it comes to the term *soul bondage,* it carries a master-slave connotation meaning; *"generally the owner or master of a servant or slave."*[12] When speaking of soul bondage, we are talking about the mastery of a soul, ownership of a soul, and a soul submitting to the demands and commands of a master. Soul bondage has a soul-slave and a soul-master, no matter how evident or apparent it may be for the individuals.

Example: Imagine a father goes to tuck his son into bed. As he looks at his son, he notices a huge lump on the top of his head. The dad then inquires; "Where did you get that awful lump on your head?"

The son, in ignorance, replies; "What lump?"

The dad did not need to be a psychic to know that his son was hit on the head. He noticed something happened to his son, though he was not a witness to what occurred to cause the lump. Even his son could not recall what had happened, but the evidence of the lump was pointing to some sort of incident.

---

[11] Sin (v)– Hebrew word Chattah meaning; to miss the mark. The mark being His teaching and instructions.
[12] "Master" -International Standard Bible Encyclopedia

Just like the son who was unaware of the lump growing on the top of his head, we too can be bound and not aware. Some of us can be caught up in a soul mastery situation, even now, without even knowing.

The shocking revelation that will be presented is;
i. How can this happen?
ii. Who or what has this kind of influence?
iii. Who are the victims of this influence?
iv. Why isn't it recognized?
v. What areas of ignorance are allowing more people not to be set free from this kind of captivity?

The Torah does not seem to offer a law regarding *soul ties* directly[13]. However, the Torah does offer laws on handling master-slave relationships. The Torah speaks on how to handle a slave as a master, how to be handled by a master if you're a slave, and it speaks to the different criteria on how to become free from a master. If you are the type of person who loves his/her master and willingly wants to be enslaved for eternity, the Torah offers principles of order to accommodate[14]. There can be a soul tie between a master and slave, but a soul tie is not necessary for a soul to be bound in a master-slave

---

[13] Commands on soul ties indirectly could be commands concerning idolatry, but that's being presumptuous.
[14] Laws of Moses concerning slavery – Naves Topical Bible "servant".
Ex 21:1-11,20-21,26-27,32; Le 19:20-22; 25:6,10,35-55; De 15:12,14,18; 24:7

relationship. A person can be bound to the very thing they hate, whereas with soul ties, the basis of it is friendship and intimacy.

> *Note: These are the types of principles in the Torah you will see being used to connect to soul bondage. Moving forward, I will offer a principle to examine from the Torah, then associate it with spiritual application for deliverance.*

Slavery is a common practice in life, whether we recognize it or not, it is present in every society. Through submitting our wills to individuals, we can potentially become their property. Just like the son who went to bed not knowing or recalling bumping his head, in the same way, you could've entered a lawful bondage contract of the soul.

In what way does a person give themselves to another person, place, or thing? What has the dominating power over your will? What is the strong, looming personality seemingly dominating your life? If they call...you run. When there is trouble... it or they are the first thing to run to. Define for yourself; when you need to escape, who is the master you run to? What is the person, place, or thing you run to? This is how you can define your master.

In the Hebrew scriptures, we can find two kinds of bondage. There is strong unseen bondage, which comes by force, and then there is bondage entered willingly and knowingly, which makes it more of a servitude. The unseen bondage can happen as a result of consequence.

At the risk of going into a word study, but for the necessity of understanding, I ask that you pay close attention to these fundamental principles.

The Hebrew word for servant is *Ebed,* Hebrews Strong's #5650[15], which roots to *Abad* H5647. This is a willing and knowing type of servitude. This is when a person submits their will to consciously serve, and the decision is deliberate, not forced on them.

In contrast to *Abad* H5647, there is another *Abad,* but its reference number is H6. *Abad* H6 is the unseen bondage that can happen as a result of consequence. I will attempt to prove this as plainly as possible.

Abad H5647 and *Abad* H6 are pronounced the same (Ah-Bahd), which makes them phonetic cognates or homonyms[16]. The difference between these words is their beginning letters and their definitions. Though I am not able to prove they have the same parent root phonetically, I am willing to step out and say their meaning similarities become evident in the end. See illustration:

---

[15] For the sake of understanding and not becoming confused I chose to offer the Strongs #'s above for clarity. *Hebrew Strong's Number* will be represented by "H" further on.

[16] Homonym - a word pronounced the same as another but differing in meaning, whether spelled the same way or not

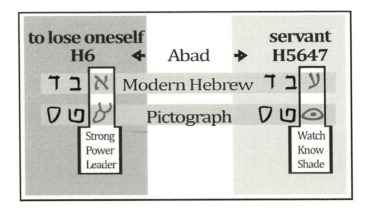

Let's examine the first letters of each word. The first letter Alef on *Abad* H6 in Hebrew word pictures represents the meaning of: Strong, Power, and Leader. The first letter Ayin on *Abad* H5647 in Hebrew word pictures represents the meaning of: Watch, Know, and Shade.

Abad H6 is defined as: to wander away, to lose oneself, lost, perish, and destruction. Looking at all 174 uses of *Abad* H6, you will notice the common usage for the word is *destroy, perish,* and *lost.* In the Ancient Hebrew Lexicon of the Bible by: Jeff A. Benner, he offers this definition:

> *A wanderer is one alone or lost. A place separated from people is a place of ruin. To be separated from the whole, life or functionality.*

When Cain killed Abel, his punishment was *Abad* H6. Genesis 4:13 states Cain mentions his punishment was greater than he can bear. The word punishment in this verse roots back to *Abad* (H6). Cain's punishment was iniquity, a perverse, crooked, moral evil established in his blood.[17]

In my studies over the years, I have learned iniquity is the connection which ties both Abad's together. The punishment of H6 *Abad* is captivity placed on you whether you like it or not. There has been actually an instance in the scriptures where the translators decided to translate the word as *no way to flee*.

The punishment of iniquity is generational. There are multiple examples in scriptures to see this. As an example, let's consider Cain, very practically.

Peshat: Cain was a farmer who worked the land for his "increase" and success. The curse given to him then causes the ground to decrease in the potential that it could produce.

> *When thou tillest the ground, it shall not henceforth yield unto thee her strength; a fugitive and a vagabond shalt thou be in the earth.*
> *Genesis 4:12 (KJV)*

---

[17] Iniquity – Hebrew word Avon H5771 – perversity, crooked, moral evil

Remez: The magnitude of this is huge when we reflect on the fact of how Adam, his father, was already handed the curse of; struggling to get the ground to produce.[18] Imagine, the one skill you have, which was hard, then it becomes harder and not as fruitful. This is how we should see the curse of Cain.

Drash: Cain's response to such a burden on his life was to abandon his trade of husbandry and build the first city of trade and commerce.

> *And Cain knew his wife; and she conceived, and bare Enoch: and he builded a city, and called the name of the city, after the name of his son, Enoch.*
> *Genesis 4:17 (KJV)*

Sud: Ask yourself where the most crime happens today? In the United States, you will notice crimes, especially murder, are greater in the cities. Urban areas and cities are the product of what a murderer devised. Areas of trade and commerce to access the "increase" that he was not able to receive from his husbandry. The spirit of the person who established it was a murderer and a pervert.

Summary: Cain was a farmer who enjoyed the increase of his land. Then, when he murdered his brother, a curse was placed on the very area where he

---

[18] Genesis 3:17-19

usually prospered. Cain's reply was; "this abad – punishment, is greater than I can bear".[19]

Though Genesis does not offer a time frame, there is a probability that Cain sowed and reaped from his land, then realized his yield had depleted. Cain was bound to this punishment. No matter the skill, the talent, or gift he offered, he was not able to "*increase*" as before. His outcome then became, in order to prosper, he would have to leave his area of trade completely.

Life application: Have you made some rash decisions in your life, and no matter what you try to do, you cannot shake the punishment of that decision? The very area that you may be gifted in never produces its strength for you. Never able to reach your maximum potential in your anointing. Then the frustration causes you to step out of your calling and anointing, only to find yourself bound to a profession outside of your gift. This is only one example of the generational effect of iniquity.

H6 Abad does mean punishment, but the punishment in the long run only becomes another bondage. A bondage is inside your soul, that is strong, torturous, and even, at times, governed by a master.

When it comes to captor/master or captive/slave relationships, recognize one can be under either strong/forceful captivity or willing/submitted captivity. Strong captivity has to do with the

---

[19] Genesis 4:13

treatment of the slave and the ability of the slave to be set free. Strong captivity can be one who was taken by force.

Example: Suppose a person in captivity was suffering from internal bleeding due to the harshness of the captivity. The symptoms of the bleeding may not be recognized, or the master may not even care about the symptoms, causing continual suffering. This would be an example of strong captivity.

Take this example of internal bleeding and replace it with the suffering of a bleeding soul whose master allows continual suffering. Compare the natural principle of internal bleeding, and then associate it with the spiritual principle of internal bleeding in your soul.

Natural: Internal bleeding may lead to a person to go into shock. **Spiritual:** A person who has not received the necessary medicinal treatment for their soul, found in the wisdom of the Torah and the Messiah, their soul too can go into shock due to bleeding internally. **Natural:** Another natural symptom of internal bleeding is a person's skin becoming cold and clammy. **Spiritual:** The captive soul which goes into shock may cause their character to become cold and clammy.

Imagine how many cold and clammy people are victims of a strong harsh bondage. Their masters may not know or even care of their internal suffering. I want to show you there is a more hands-on application that is necessary for true deliverance.

Some masters take their slaves into captivity violently, like through kidnapping, but in the context of this book, we'll call it "soul-napping." A person who has been raped or molested has been taken by force into soul bondage. The Torah offers principles, rights, and judgments to be set free from this type of strong bondage.

Sex was designed to be a covenant between a man and his wife. This is one tool used to bring them together as one soul. When a person is forced into a sexual covenant without permission, their soul becomes one with them by force. There is no way to flee a mingled soul, you will be bound.

The difference between soul bondage from a soul tie is; with a *soul tie* being *tied* does not always equate to dominance or mastery by the other soul. A clear definition for "soul ties" would be found in Deuteronomy 13:6.

> *If your brother, the son of your mother, or your son, or your daughter, or the wife of your bosom,* ***or your friend, who is as your own soul****, entice you secretly, saying, Let us go and serve other gods, which you have not known, you, nor your fathers; (WEB)*

When a lesson on soul ties is offered, religious leaders reference scriptures such as David and

Jonathan,[20] a husband and wife,[21] or a child tied at the soul of their progenitors[22]. The text of Deuteronomy 13:6 reverberates as one of many common references dealing with soul ties.

From the statement in Deuteronomy, we can see the Most High[23] does not say someone tied to your soul is a sin. It seems the problem comes when someone takes advantage of the soul connection to use it as obligation or mastery. Every *soul tie* is not a soul bondage, and every *Soul Bondage* is not a soul tie.

"Soul ties" are limited to another soul, whereas with soul bondages, the captivity can be with:

-Nouns (person, places, or things) – Example: Feeling a necessity to be in a certain "building" to have fulfillment.

-Pronouns (substitutes for nouns and noun phrases, and have a very general reference, as I, you, he, this, who, her, what) - Example: A person could be experiencing shame of the person they have submitted to or is in strong bondage to, so they use terms which will only infer to them versus calling the person out by name. This is done either consciously or subconsciously. If the person stated the name, it would remind the listener and speaker of the

---

[20] I Sam. 18:1
[21] Genesis 2:24
[22] Genesis 44:30
[23] The Most High – Often referred to as the Most High God, Elohim the power. These is a universal, generic term. Commonly translated as God and LORD. Also interchangeable with YHWH, Yah, YahoWah, Yahuah, Yahweh, Yehowah and on.

character of the slave's master. Phrases like; "He should be picking me up" are used instead of saying their name. This has a strong root in shame. Dare someone challenge the speaker with the reply; "He who?"

-Adjectives (describing a particular quality of a word) – These individuals may be in bondage to the attributes of a master or slave. Example: A person who is tall, dark, and handsome. Because someone possesses these attributes, one may choose to stay bound, or become bound. On the other hand, a person may be put into captivity by an individual because of those desired attributes, caring less about the individual themselves.

-Verbs (reveals what is happening, usually action) – This is a person in bondage or putting others into bondage due to their actions. Statements like; "She had me as soon as I saw her dance." Dare anyone ask; what was her name? Who is she as a person? It was all about the dance or action she displayed.

Mastery rooted in obligation has crippled homes, gangs, families, organizations, communities, friendships, marriages, churches, and many more. How many people remain in prison due to an oath[24] or vow[25] of loyalty, while their master continues on freely with their lives? How many people die on

---

[24] "Oath" – To yoke a binding agreement including the curse for violating the oath. Hebrews Strong's # 7621 and 423
[25] "Vow" - Promises to perform an act if another performs a certain act. Hebrews Strong's #H2385

sinking ships or decay with dying movements due to the mastery of some leader or their idea?

Yes, you can be mastered by an idea, yet an idea is not tangible. Just from these few examples, you can see the unlimited possibilities mastery offers versus a friendship or soul tie.

You can continue to read as one in bondage to a master or as a master who has souls in submission. You may even know someone who is a *master* soul enslaver, or you could be in a situation where you are being mastered by someone. No matter what the perspective is, this revelation is a necessary tool to effectively help friends and family around you.

Four

SLAVES TO INFIRMITY

Paul shows us we are going to be slaves to the Messiah or we are going to be slaves to sin.

> *Know ye not, that to whom ye yield yourselves servants to obey, his servants ye are to whom ye obey; whether of sin unto death, or of obedience unto righteousness? But God be thanked, that ye were the servants of sin, but ye have obeyed from the heart that form of doctrine which was delivered you. Being then made free from sin, ye became the servants of righteousness.*
> *Romans 6:16-18 (KJV)*

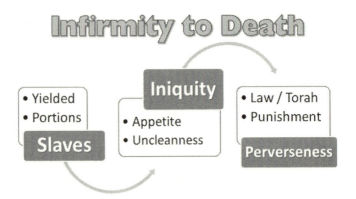

> *I speak after the manner of men because of **the infirmity of your flesh**: for as ye have **yielded your members servants** to **uncleanness** and to **iniquity** unto **iniquity**; even so now yield your members servants to righteousness unto holiness.*
> *Romans 6:19 (KJV)*

Romans offers a depreciation that begins with something as harmless as uncleanness, which then leads to iniquity[26] unto iniquity, but the concern of Paul was the infirmity. He began way back in chapter one talking about the firmness needed in faith already being established by him. Then after their conversion, the community yielded to a weakness called infirmity.

Infirmity is an adjective that describes a state of being or the status. The status being described is not

---

[26] Iniquity – Sins passed down from the father, gross injustice.

being firm in faith or character. Not being strong or solidly fixed in place is the state of infirmity.

When a woman is going through her menstruation cycle, it is considered a state/status of unclean. Unclean is not a sin, and neither is infirmity. The common denominator is the need to transition from these states or statuses.

Uncleanness is not about being dirty or filthy. Uncleanness is about your ability to flow in the Most High's movement on the earth.

A person can be in a state or status without transitioning for years...bound. If the opportunity presents itself for them to transition yet they choose to remain bound in that status, then it can become sin.

Example: The Torah offers a woman to transition from her uncleanness once her time is fulfilled. She can then offer the appropriate sin offering and transition.[27] In the story of *the woman with the issue of blood,* in the gospels, she had this infirmity for twelve years.[28] Her opportunity to transition had not come for twelve years until Y'shua comes along, and by her faith, she became whole.[29] Now that her time was fulfilled, the transitional sin-offering was possible.

A sin-offering was prescribed according to the Torah not because she knowingly did something wrong but because she unwittingly came into

---

[27] Leviticus 15:30;
[28] Luke 8:43-44; Mark 5:25-27; Matthew 9:20-21;
[29] Luke 8:48

uncleanness and now needed to transition back into clean. Remember, uncleanness is not about being dirty or filthy. Uncleanness is about your ability to flow in the Most High's movement on the earth. This is very important to remember moving forward in the examples ahead. The picture of uncleanness in Hebrew is the picture of a basket holding water.[30] This is still water, not flowing, but stagnant water.

When the Most High used his mobile moving tabernacle in the wilderness, it allowed Israel an opportunity to connect with the father. Today, we also have an opportunity to connect with the Most High via His *Set-Apart Spirit*. The prerequisite set in *Leviticus 15:31* is that when you are unclean, then choose not to transition from uncleanness, attempting to function in His movement is defilement with the penalty of death.

> *Thus shall ye separate the children of Israel from their uncleanness; that they die not in their uncleanness, when they defile my tabernacle that is among them.*
> *Leviticus 15:31 (KJV)*

Infirmity is a weakness or feebleness in your soul that allows HaSatan[31] an opportunity to siphon your anointing, your potential, and providence. This keeps

---

[30] Hebrew Strong's #2930; Tame AHL defined
[31] "HaSatan" – the adversary - often translated as Satan

you bound to a state of lack; spiritually, emotionally, and financially.

Paul speaks to his family of converts called the Romans. These are people *in* the Messiah, not people who *need* the Messiah. They have unwittingly or wittingly come into a state of infirmity. Without the wisdom to transition from the *status* of infirmity, they could've found themselves bound to even greater consequences.

The illustration shows the context of Romans 6:19.

> ... *because of the infirmity of your flesh: for as ye have yielded your members servants to uncleanness and to iniquity unto iniquity; even so now yield your members servants to righteousness unto holiness...*

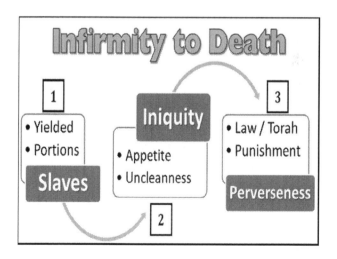

1. Section one: ...*for as ye have yielded your members servants*... Another way of saying what Paul offered is *that by the submission of our members to be slaves.*

These members can be any portion of our flesh we allow or submit as slaves, often translated as servants. When we submit our eyes (members) to what is evil, we then give that *evil* permission to cleave or bind itself to our soul. As said in Psalms 101:3;

> *I will set no wicked thing before mine eyes: I hate the work of them that turn aside; it shall not* ***cleave to me***. *(KJV)*

2. Section two: ...*to uncleanness*... After the submission of our members to our new captors, Paul offers we now come into a status of uncleanness. Without the appropriate transition from the uncleanness, whether natural, emotional, or spiritual, we can trigger our sinful appetite.

Principles in Action: Like in the example in section one; once we have realized our eyes have seen something unclean that pollutes our soul, we need to transition. Physically wash, and ask the Messiah to cleanse our inward parts, spiritually.[32] Submit to the wisdom of Ruach HaKodesh for understanding and

---

[32] Messiah as the water that cleanses our soul can be found in – John 4:10-16 and John 7:37-39

self-examination of where there might have been a violation or trigger to prevent it from happening again. Bathe your inward parts with the reading of His scriptures. Receive the atoning work of Y'shua and do not walk in condemnation. The wisdom of His spirit should offer the appropriate reflective repentance, so the same mistake is not repeated. Accept the recompense with humility, with the goal of moving forward. Boldly throw yourself on the throne room floor for mercy.

HaSatan knows our sinful flesh carries the propensity to sin. His desire is to activate or even establish a sinful appetite in our soul.

Example: Imagine if a person had never experienced the taste of ice cream with all the toppings you usually enjoy. Being that they never had a chance to experience the ice cream how you like it, they are not able to establish a craving for what you enjoy.

HaSatan's attempt is to offer you an opportunity to establish a craving for sin that you should have never been exposed to. This perverting of the soul is the markers, seeds, the polluting, and beginnings of soul bondage.

A man who exposes himself to a young child is an agent of HaSatan sent to the young child to pervert their soul. HaSatan's goal is to establish a point of ownership in the blood, so in the later years of their life, they have more of a potential to crave the same type of debauchery or pornographic material. Remember, all this is from the triggered appetite of uncleanness. As stated before, soul bondage can be either by force, strong captivity, or by willing submission.

... *and to iniquity*...Paul offers that the uncleanness we are exposed to can lead to iniquity. Paul uses iniquity here in the context of a noun (person, place, or thing) and as a verb (action). I have learned the iniquity noun is what drives the iniquity verb. Like appetite, it too is a driving force.

Iniquity (noun) is the *why* behind the actions of iniquity (verb)/sin. Since sin is missing the mark[33] and transgression is knowingly committing acts of sin in rebellion,[34] iniquity (noun) is the transgressions passed down from generation to generation[35].

Through the submission of our members to uncleanness, an appetite is established that potentially wasn't even known to be there. When a soul chooses not to transition, that is when the iniquity (noun) of the fathers comes collecting on the sin debt caused by the previous transgressions in the blood. The iniquity (noun) acted upon becomes the iniquity (verb).

Example: Continuing with the scenario we have going from section one. The eyes (members) became

---

[33] Chattah #H2401 – An offense. Error -AHL #H2402 #H2403 - An act or condition of ignorant or imprudent deviation from a code of behavior. A missing of the target in the sense of making a mistake.
[34] Transgression #H6586 – Rebellion. To sin with an high hand. Intentional sin.
[35] Exodus 20:5 ... visiting the iniquity of the fathers upon the children unto the third and fourth generation of them that hate me;

exposed to pornographic material, not by choice, but someone showed them an adult magazine. After the soul looks out of curiosity, submission, the recognition that is unclean causes the feeling of sin-guilt. Choosing not to transition, the soul looks harder, the iniquity then begins to be established.

As time goes on, the soul is now an individual who lurks behind buildings where the same type of pornographic material is being sold.

The actions are iniquity (verb); the actions of wickedness. Because there still wasn't a transition when the iniquity (noun) came calling, the continuance in the infirmity led to iniquity (verb). At the point when iniquity (noun) presented itself was the opportunity to distinguish between life and death, via the Torah, then to choose life. If a soul isn't aware of the iniquity (noun) and is not able to distinguish between life and death, failure is more likely. I am talking about falling into iniquity (verb). This is the beauty of the Torah, because it is the knowledge of sin.[36] As a person studies the laws, statutes and judgments of the Torah, they become more sensitive to sin. The ability to discern the difference between death and life become keen.[37]

---

[36] Romans 3:20

[37] Wisdom – Is your ability to discern difference, specifically the difference between right and wrong. Then Deuteronomy 4:6 says the Torah "is your wisdom and your understanding in the sight of the nations"

> *Yet say ye, Why? doth not the son bear the iniquity of the father? When the son hath done that which is lawful and right, and hath kept all my statutes, and hath done them, he shall surely live. Ezekiel 18:19 (KJV)*

3. Section Three: *...unto iniquity...* Now Paul offers *iniquity unto iniquity* which we refer to as iniquity punishment. Iniquity punishment is another bondage that can have a soul trapped for a lifetime. The first time we see iniquity used in this form is in Genesis chapter four, dealing with the curse of Cain.

> *And Cain said unto the LORD, My **punishment** is greater than I can bear. Genesis 4:13 (KJV)*

The word punishment used in Genesis 4:13 is the Hebrew word used for iniquity.[38] This is what Paul was showing the Romans, when he wrote iniquity (verb) will lead to iniquity punishment.

Section three shows how once the actions of iniquity are carried out, then the law/Torah has an appropriate recompense for the iniquity action committed. Since the law/Torah governs the earth, when an action of iniquity is committed, the law/Torah judges those said actions and issues a verdict, more specifically in this context, a

---
[38] Punishment / Iniquity - #H5771 Avon

punishment. What is the punishment for iniquity? Paul was able to deduce from the Torah the punishment for iniquity is more iniquity.

The judgment is being left to yourself trying to find a way out of the bondage trap you created, only to find that every opportunity to leave the bondage is sabotaged by your own self.

> *In meekness instructing **those that oppose themselves**; if God peradventure will give them repentance to the acknowledging of the truth;*
> ***And that they may recover themselves out of the snare of the devil, who are taken captive by him at his will**.*
> 2 Timothy 2:25-26

Paul statements in 2 Timothy 2:25-26 alludes to the point. A soul opposing themselves is a soul bound only to sabotage their own deliverance. Paul instructs Timothy not to snatch them out of captivity, but to *instruct them into deliverance.*

Iniquity is perversion,[39] it is the twisting of truth. The same truth designed to set a soul free becomes twisted and distorted. It is like seeing an escape hatch but talking oneself out of taking it.

Example: Continuing our established example from section 1-2: A soul is now looking at pornographic material behind a building. The penalty

---

[39] Perversion / Iniquity - #H5771 Avon

is more iniquity. As the soul continues in the lifestyle of depravity, they find themselves unsatisfied with magazines, so now the iniquity needs movies.

The soul starts with soft-core pornography but becomes un-fulfilled, so the iniquity needs hardcore pornography. The hardcore, after some time, becomes un-stimulating, so the now perverted soul needs weird, strange, fetish pornography. This bondage only gets worse until the soul begins acting out the gross injustice it has seen its master do. The slave to iniquity then becomes a pervert only stimulated through exhibitionism. Bringing full circle, the seed planted when they were violated.

> *Note: Though it may sound like a far jump from watching pornography to exposing yourself to children, I just want you to consider the seed can only produce after its own kind. The master demonic force over that soul demands production and increase of other souls. At the root of the perversion of watching pornography is voyeurism. So, how is does a voyeurism seed to get planted? Exactly. The defilement of another soul has to happen. How do you defile a soul into watching sexual acts? By exposing it to sexual acts, whether willing or by force.*

Remember, the perversion of the iniquity keeps a soul bound. When the opportunity to escape the bondage was presented, the perverted soul twisted the opening or opportunity. These openings and opportunities to escape are the wisdom and grace of the Torah.[40] These small openings are small reprieves to escape or think soberly.

Proverbs says; perverseness is like a breach in the spirit. Think about a person bound within themselves, and when someone offers them an escape, they get distracted, uninterested, tired, car troubles, called in for work, etc. These are all the fruit of infirmity, because they have not the firmness or fortitude to stand against their own selves.

Infirmity is another way HaSatan keeps our soul in bondage. Because of bitterness, soul perversion, unforgiveness, wounds and breaches in our spirit, the full functionality that it could reach is not attained.

Infirmity Caused by Emotional and Spiritual Conflict

A man who has experienced emotional trauma from fighting in a war can be bound by the wounds in his soul. Constant reminders of the memories tormenting him, which, at times, can be a physical wound, loss of a loved one, a tangible smell or taste that triggers memories. This can cause an emotional and spiritual conflict.

---

[40] Grace - an allowance of time after a debt or bill has become payable granted to the debtor before suit can be brought against him or her or a penalty applied: - Dictionary.com Unabridged. Random House, Inc. 09 Jun. 2016

Emotional and spiritual conflict is internal conflict in a soul. When a soul is trained or exposed to do acts against their natural design or against the will of the Father, the conflict begins. Acts not of love but acts that go against the core fiber of their soul's conscience. It can be a conflict against your destiny or providence. These acts create a wound, a breach, and an access point in the soul for HaSatan to torment internally. This conflict then leads to infirmity.

Infirmity is the sickness or disease keeping souls bound. **Example:** A person can go on a cruise for a ten-day vacation, but while out at sea, feel the demand and tug on their soul to return home to their captors. Their captors are family, friends, loved ones, an over demanding job...the very thing they planned the vacation for, now tugs at them. This torment may seem subtle at first, then as the days increase, the torment becomes greater and greater. This can cause an individual to go to the captain of the ship and express their need to turn the boat around etc. This is evidence of infirmity. What if you are not aware of the principles of the Torah to see this when it happens?

This is the reason why Y'shua lets us know we can only have one master.

> *No man can serve two masters: for either he will hate the one and love the other; or else he will hold to the one and despise the other. Ye cannot serve God and mammon.*
> *Matthew 6:24 (KJV)*

Infirmity is torment to the soul. There are people waiting for deliverers who can set them free from the internal struggle that is happening within them.

The emotional and spiritual conflict that leads to infirmity is best described as an internal struggle within yourself, with no sure win in sight. When you have feelings of hate, while at the same time love, this is an emotional and spiritual conflict. When you have a desire to do right, but an appetite to do wrong, this is an emotional and spiritual conflict. When you are torn between your convictions and external/carnal circumstances, this is an emotional and spiritual conflict.

Paul shows us a remedy to overcome this turmoil in Romans chapter 7-8. Christians have missed the power of Paul's wisdom to the Romans. Most Christians use these verses as an excuse to remain in their perversion, but that is the fruit of their infirmity. Infirmity is a very sad state to be tormented with. Yet, your master doesn't want you to go free.

Through the principles of the Torah, the chronicles of Y'shua, and New covenant writers, you can learn freedom from this *master infirmity*. Infirmity causes an internal back and forth with no purpose to grasp onto. It is a state of having a carnal view of the world with no peace. It can be a person, place, thing, food, family, attitudes, ideas, laziness, depression, emotional or spiritual bonds.

> *For to be carnally minded is death; but to be spiritually minded is life and peace.*
> *Romans 8:6 (KJV)*

We want to make sure that you do not confuse the precepts of being double-minded with infirmity. The distinction between the two precepts can be distinguished by words like; goal, purpose, and destination. A double-minded person is one without a goal, a purpose, or a destination. James says; the double-minded is *a wave of the sea* driven with the wind and tossed.[41] Not a boat on the sea with a goal or destination, nor a swimmer in the sea, but *the wave* itself.

Infirmity is when there is a goal, a purpose and a destination in mind. Using those two definitions; we can say infirmity is the boat with a captain and goal, while being double-minded is the waves smashing against the boat. When a person focuses more on the waves and not the destination and allows the waves

---

[41] Wave of sea – James 1:6

to distract them from the destination, that is when infirmity begins to increase towards death.

Here are some practical examples from the Torah where infirmity is caused by an emotional and spiritual conflict.

Isaac had to pray to the Most High to deliver his wife from barrenness.[42] As a result of the prayer, not only did she get pregnant, but she conceived twins. The struggle of the twins inside her womb was so bad that she inquired from other women and elders. [43] She finally went to the Most High to ask why there was a struggle in her womb.[44]

How many times do we go to our family and friends about their infirmity they are struggling with, yet it only ends in confrontation? They become offended because you see their infirmity, but they also see it too, but do not have the keys necessary to set themselves free.

The Most High answers Rebekah and lets her know there are two nations in her womb, and that the younger born will be the greater, not as the usual custom of giving honor to the eldest. This is special; the younger shall rule the older.

We can imagine that she tried to keep it to herself, but her closest family, friends, community network, and husband surely had to have drawn the news of the prophecy given to her. But, suppose they did not draw it out of her, or she never told. This

---

[42] Genesis 25:21
[43] Book of Yasher Chapter 26:9-12
[44] Genesis 25:23

would be the building blocks for infirmity. Inside her, the conversation would have been:

> *On one side it is great news that I now know what is going on with my body, but on the other side, I can't tell the men and the other heads of the community how the Most High calls for the younger to be elevated as if he is the oldest.*

This is how simple it is to get caught in an emotional and spiritual conflict. The back and forth of feelings versus principles, fear versus faith, love versus hate, and principle versus love.

You may say to yourself, *I'm 34 years old, it's not that bad, I have it under control.* But this is the trap of the sickness, it perverts and warps your thinking.

Fast forward, Jacob is now born as the youngest to his twin brother Esau. The scripture says;

> *And Isaac loved Esau, because he did eat of his venison: but Rebekah loved Jacob.*
> *Genesis 25:28 (KJV)*

Jacob's mom is trying to groom him to walk in an anointing that he may or may not have any clue he was called to walk in. The Father who is supposed to be the real visionary of the home, was too busy focusing on his elder son's carnal accomplishments.[45]

This is another example of a spiritual and emotional conflict. Jacob, in his soul, understands the appropriate function of a father would be to sow vision into him, as a son. Yet his own brother, who looks just like him, gets the attention. Jacob knows that his father is completely capable of loving him as much as he loves Esau but this is not the case.

Infirmity presents itself as real, but once you zoom the camera lens out, you can see its all fake. A person may feel trapped in a box with no escape possible, yet the bigger picture shows that there are so many other avenues. A soul can feel like a person murdered, laying on a white kitchen floor, while the whole time, the Most High's plan for them is to be soaring in the clouds with the eagles.

These are minor examples from the story of Jacob, but as you read his story, the infirmity and emotional and spiritual conflict is constantly seen throughout his timeline. As you look at each person's story from their perspective, hopefully you will be able to see the emotional and spiritual conflict. Esau hating the very person who he looks like. Esau had to look in the mirror and see a face that he hates yet, try to love himself.

Keys to Deliverance: Paul took a very simple principle like slavery and related back to our walk

---

[45] Genesis 25:28

with the Messiah. He was saying (paraphrased); *if you served sin by submitting your will to the sin, now serve Christ by submitting your will to Christ.*

Of course, this is easier said than done. Paul then offers a vision of what the result will be if you submit to Christ:

> *But now being made free from sin, and become servants to God, ye have your fruit unto holiness, and the end everlasting life. For the wages of sin is death; but the gift of God is eternal life through Jesus Christ our Lord.*
> *Romans 6:22-23 (KJV)*

Then in your mind, you may say; *But you just don't know the struggle that is going on inside me. When I want to do right, I don't. Then the wrong that I do not want to do, I find myself always doing it.*[46]

Here is your deliverance!! According to the Torah[47], whenever a woman marries a man, she is bound to him, but if he dies, she is no longer bound to him.[48] This is our out!! Just like in death you are free from the connection with your spouse in the same manner is it with sin. If we die to sin, we are no

---

[46] Romans 7:14-24
[47] Deuteronomy 25:5; Genesis 2:23-24
[48] Romans 7:2

longer under the bondage of *Master Sin*. BUT!! Being dead alone is not enough. We must resurrect in the newness of life. Not trying to imitate *religious* behaviors but serving him in the newness of spirit.[49]

A person who is bound in a state of infirmity, as shown earlier, sabotages their own deliverance, producing a cycle of shame, guilt, and disappointment. Then any effort to be set free seems futile. This is the lie. While some will have you learn to live with your state of infirmity, the Most High has not destined that for you. Science will offer you therapy to become a better you, while the Kingdom of Yah accepts no reformed only the transformed.

The transformation begins when you decide in all your being that you hate the state you are in. Then stop attempting to set yourself free through religious actions. Allow and yield to the spirit of Christ, taking the only course of action that He tells you. This is walking after the Spirit.[50] *Romans 8:5-9 says;*

For they that are after the flesh do mind the things of the flesh; but they that are after the Spirit the things of the Spirit. For to be carnally minded is death; but to be spiritually minded is life and peace. <u>*Because the carnal mind is enmity against God: for it is not subject to the law of God, neither indeed can be.*</u> *So then they that are in the flesh cannot please God. But ye are not in the flesh, but in the Spirit, if so*

---

[49] Romans 7:6
[50] Romans 8:3-4

be that the Spirit of God dwell in you. Now if any man have not the Spirit of Christ, he is none of his.

Paul said to be carnally minded is hatred toward Elohim. Anything that cannot transcend into Heaven is considered carnal. These are tangible, earthly items that your mind inflates their importance over YHWH[51]. Your job, your marriage, your children, your house, your cars, are all examples of tangible carnal things. The carnal world must lose all its value, and you must become dead to it. Then as you submit all your members to the Spirit of Messiah, you then begin to cross-over into the realm of the spiritual.

The Torah of righteousness is spiritual, and we are carnal, only when we walk the principals of the Torah in the Spirit of Messiah will it not equal death[52]. One more time, the spiritual Torah is for spiritual people. The only way you can be spiritual is if you are dead to the carnal and resurrected in the newness of his spirit.

Think about it, you will no longer live on the roller coaster of infirmity. You will become sensitive to His will not your flesh's will. The bondage that used to enslave, now becomes the testimony to set others free. It all starts with a decision. You don't need a preacher or some religious leader to tell you what to say. Throw yourself on the mercy of the court

---

[51] YHWH – tetragrammaton for the sacred name of The Most High God. YahWeh, Yahuah, Yehowah, Yahovah etc.
[52] Romans 7:14

and ask Father to begin to trust you with His commands. Hate the carnal and look forward toward the promise of life.

> *Nay, in all these things we are more than conquerors through him that loved us. For I am persuaded, that neither death, nor life, nor angels, nor principalities, nor powers, nor things present, nor things to come, Nor height, nor depth, nor any other creature, shall be able to separate us from the love of God, which is in Christ Jesus our Lord.*
> *Romans 8:37-39 (KJV)*

Five

DEFINING A SOUL

Looking back on my life being raised in the Christian Charismatic movement, there was always justification toward sin. Phrases like "hate the sin, but love the sinner," "No one is perfect, we are all sinners," were common phrases I would hear.

These kept my soul perverted and bound to sin. The schism in my mind was created that there was this alter entity in me that I was just going to have to be bound to for life. As silly as it sounds now, but my perversion had me thinking my soul was evil, but my spirit was good. These two then fought for control over my flesh. Most of this was probably rooted in the *Trinity thinking* Christians often teach.

This is another bondage of the soul. Not being free within your person but bound to perversion. It would be like dragging the old dead man around with you everywhere you go, only causing you to fall back into uncleanness. The Hebrew understanding of soul is what I want to share with you.

Is your soul "evil" or just not trained? Characteristics that are your carnal mind often become attributed to your soul. The carnal mind is an unruly child that will never submit to order.[53] Like a child has a natural appetite to be fed from birth, your soul too has a natural appetite. But your carnal mind is not your soul. Though one of the things they have in common is an appetite. One of the definitions for soul in the Hebrew is "*appetite*."[54]

Now, my attempt at defining a soul is not to give you the readily available information found by simply looking up the word "soul" in any encyclopedia. I want to offer the revelations for its function to aid each person toward understanding your soul's function.

If one of the definitions for the word soul is appetite, is appetite merely evil? No. The appetite in all soul creations is not evil. It seems when the appetite masters a creature does it have the potential of being evil. When it exists in a manner of dysfunction from its intended purpose, then it has the potential of being evil.

From creation, Adam was not evil nor was he dysfunctional. It is only when he went outside the parameters of his intended purpose that it allowed

---

[53] Romans 8:7
[54] "Soul" – #H5315 nephesh

wickedness to enter the soul of man. One of the misconceptions is; the soul is an evil force fighting against a righteous will in a person. In the Hebrew, though, there is no dualism[55] present. There is not an evil you and good you. There is only one you.

Soul is also defined as *"person."*[56] Saying *"soul"* is synonymous with saying *"person."* You, as a person, cannot be separated from your soul. If your soul is evil, then you, as a person, must be evil as well. *"Good trees bear good fruit and corrupt trees bear evil fruit."*[57] Y'shua puts it even more plainly when he states;

> *"If you then, being evil, know how to give good gifts to your children, how much more will your heavenly Father give the Holy Spirit to those who ask him?" Luke 11:13 (WEB)*

Yes, we as people, are souls. Everything attributed to an individual as a *"person"* is soul. Ancestors, descendants, life, self, it is all soul. In Exodus 1:5, the Scriptures list all the descendants of Israel and labels them as "Souls."

---

[55] "Dualism" - The conjunction of two (usually opposing) entities or principles. The Concise Oxford Dictionary of World Religions 1997
[56] "Soul" – #H5315 nephesh
[57] Matthew 7:17

> *And all the souls that came out of the loins of Jacob were seventy souls: for Joseph was in Egypt already. (KJV)*

I want to stress this point to ensure we are not trying to assign character traits to another entity outside or inside of ourselves. Soul in Hebrew thought is the whole unit of a person. There is not a second evil entity inside a person called *"soul."* The doctrine idea of; *"loving the sinner but hate the sin"* has caused the perversion in people to think there is a schism from the evil actions and the evil person. It's just the opposite. Evil people do evil things, not good people possessing evil ways. A person's soul is not the source of the problem; a person is soul. If a person is a soul, then your "person" must be the source of the evil. As pointed out above, your ancestry is in your soul. Maybe these evils are the inherited evils of your progenitors. Either way, we must all take responsibility for the evils encompassing our person.

A body ceases to be a person when there is no longer a soul in it. At this point, your body is just a physical structure. In Hebrew, the word body is defined as *a sheath for the soul.*[58] When a news broadcast reports on a murder, the wording used is *"...the body was found."* When the soul is within the body, we have a complete person. When the soul leaves the body, there is no longer a person but only

---

[58] "Body"- #H5085 nidneh

an outer shell left. This is just a simple example to prove unity of soul and body.

When the Most High breathed into mankind, he became a *"living soul."*[59] Not just an instinctive appetite pattern, which resonates in animals, but *"a whole complete person, the body, breath and mind."*[60] The Most High formed humankind after the likeness of his own image. This is the uniqueness of the human soul. There is an animalistic, instinctive, beastly, appetite present, but the Most High gave us a soul of will, a likeness of Himself, full of choices and spirit.

The soul is housed in the blood[61]. Breath is also present in the blood, and even though the soul is intangible, blood itself is completely tangible. These complexities of the word soul alone have baffled theologians and philosophers for centuries.

Understand, I'm not trying to give a concrete definition, but instead, offer another view outside Trinitarianism[62] and Dualism, permeating our societies thought. This causes individuals to not take responsibility for themselves, i.e. soul and actions.

Breath in Hebrew is defined as spirit; it is also seen as soul. This really trims down the possibilities of a three-person theory often suggested by the

---

[59] Genesis 2:7 - vayhi ha adam lenefesh chaya
[60] #H2424 "Living Soul" - Ancient Hebrew Lexicon (AHL) of the Bible by Jeff A. Benner | 2010
[61] Leviticus 17:11
[62] "Trinitarianism" – Belief in the trinity by which God is considered as existing in three persons. The Columbia Encyclopedia, 6th ed. | 2016 Copyright The Columbia University Press.

Trinitarians. Imagine the chaos inside your person if you had three individuals with their own thoughts and opinions trying to run you.

In the Hebrew Scriptures, the human being is a single and undivided entity; the soul and body are not clearly distinguished from one another.[63]

The *desires*[64] and *passions*[10] of man are seated in the soul. Can you attest to hearing stories where these desires and passions of a person have raged out of control to the point of violence and atrocities?

The type of soul that commits vile crimes would be called "evil." I'm not trying to take away from the responsibility of evil nor justify these crimes, but who trained that soul? Since the appetite of an *animal*[8] is in us from birth, maybe the so-called "evil soul" has never been trained, disciplined, or reared. Now the evil soul is more spoiled and unruly. Just think of a child who has never had proper authority or structure; a soul without reasoning.

The Most High offers a remedy for the unruly soul, found in the principles of the Torah. Since the soul is person and character, the battle of HaSatan is for the possession of persons and our character. If a person assimilates into the attributes of an animalistic, instinctive, appetite-driven, unruly beast, then they have taken on the characteristics of beast, or should I say, "the beast." When we allow ourselves to live in the attributes of the animalistic soul, we are

---

[63] "Soul" - The Oxford Companion to the Body | 2001
[64] "Desires and Passions"– #H5315 nephesh

allowing ourselves to walk in nature outside the will of the Most High.

Sud: The book of Revelation states; the soul who takes on the characters of the beast is like worshipping the beast or submitting to the beast. Revelation 13:17 and 14:11 has the phrase "name of the beast" and "mark of his name."

"Name" in Hebrew describes character *(found in the word Shem H8034).* The text could easily read as "character of the beast" and "mark of his character." The character of man is the soul of the man. How you handle your soul; what you allow yourself to be in bondage to could determine your eternal destiny.

While some may be concerned about taking on the mark of the beast, at the same time, you may want to consider; you can take on the character of the beast and be just as doomed. Resist the mark, yes, but also be set free from the character of the beast.

The Intangible Soul

A soul is a non-material or non-tangible part of a person that is the central location of his/her personality, intellect, emotions, and will; the human spirit. Most religions teach that the soul lives on after the death of the body.[65]

---

[65] "Soul" - World Encyclopedia 2005, originally published by Oxford University Press 2005

If the soul is seen as the *intangible you*, all the functions attributed to a tangible person's functions are now attributed to the intangible you, *soul*. A soul thinks and speaks apart from your brain and functioning body.[66]

How many people have stopped to think that even while your mouth is closed, your soul can still be speaking to another soul in the room? In Genesis chapter 4:10, it says; the blood, or soul, of Abel cried from the ground.

> *And he said, what hast thou done?* ***the voice of thy brother's blood crieth*** *unto me from the ground. (KJV)*

I can remember when I was a child, I would go outside and play with my friends. When it became time for me to come back into the house, my mother would scream from inside the door for me to come in. The house itself was not screaming but my mother inside the house.

As stated before, the soul is housed in the blood. This was Able's soul crying from the ground. Because we are not able to see *soul*, imagining a soul crying from the ground would only allow us to see the ground. The ground did not cry though. This had to have been the soul of Abel crying out for justice.

One of the principles we can take away from this text is our intangible soul has a voice. It screams,

---

[66] Genesis 4:10

shouts, and cries into the intangible and tangible world. Today, when your soul cries out or speaks up, what is it saying? Who is it calling out to?

The intangible soul of a person can be transferred and intermingled with other souls.[67] A soul can separate from the body, travel, linger and hover through methods of Astro-projection or as some call it an *out of body experience*.[68] [69] It can become tired and weary[70], grieved[71], and even depressed[72]. These are just some, to name a few, of the intangible possible characteristics of the soul.

Someone may not be able to grab an emotion, but another person can definitely pick it up. The intangible character traits of the soul have led the American Tract Society Dictionary to write:

> *This must be spiritual, because it thinks; it must be immortal, because it is spiritual.*

The soul has been attributed as being the inner flesh[73] of man. This offers more understanding to why Y'shua would state in Matthew 10:28;

---

[67] See previous section on "soul ties"
[68] "Astro-projection" - Webster's New Millennium Dictionary of English, Preview Edition (v 0.9.7). June 2008
[69] "Astro-projection" – 2 Corinthians 12:2
[70] "Tired and weary" - Job 10:1; Psalm 6:6
[71] "Grieved" - Job 30:20-25
[72] "Depressed" - Psalm 42:5, 11; 43:5
[73] "Inner Flesh" – #H7607 – Sheh'er

> *And fear not them which kill the body but are not able to kill the soul: but rather fear him which is able to destroy both soul and body in hell. (KJV)*

Though the soul is intangible and in the inner part of man, Y'shua offers it can be destroyed, but only by "him which is able." Since the Most High informed us in Ezekiel 18:4 that *"All souls"* are His, being he is the creator of all, certainly, He would be the only one able to destroy a soul.

Souls in the intangible heavenlies show us characteristics we have been accustomed to knowing in the tangible, such as speaking, emotions, feeling, breathing, dancing, and consciences. Hebrews 11:4 goes as far as to say; *"he (meaning Abel), being dead, still speaks."* This gives us a clue of the intangible, yet spiritual soul, still holding these attributes even after physical death.

A soul residing in hell or in the heavenlies has all their senses intact. Would it be too drastic to challenge ourselves to consider even the Most High having a soul? He has a seat of emotions, yet is pure and set-apart, having passions and desires, but still in a harmonic order.

> *And I will set my tabernacle among you: and **my soul** shall not abhor you. Leviticus 26:11 (KJV)*

Tangible Effects on the Intangible Soul

Those were some of the intangible characteristics of a soul, but does this mean the tangible world cannot affect the functionality of an intangible soul? Are we to assume because you can't grasp a soul in your palm, slapping a person with that same palm would not affect a soul?

Hopefully, the foundation for a soul being a person has been established. A soul can be pure or defiled. A soul can be wicked or righteous. A soul can be stained, tarnished, and twisted (confused), bitter, darkened, and scarred. When a person receives a scar on their flesh, the soul documents it.

All these examples of characteristics of the soul are found in the Torah. Paul states:

> *To the pure all things are pure: but unto them that are defiled and unbelieving is nothing pure; but even their mind and conscience is defiled.*
> *Titus 1:15 (KJV)*

Therefore, as a person endures a trauma,[74] so will a soul. These traumatic events in our lives have lasting effects on our character/soul, our being/soul, and how we relate to others around us.

---

[74] "Trauma" – a body wound or shock produced by sudden physical injury, as from violence or accident. 2. -an experience that produces psychological injury or pain. Dictionary.com Unabridged. Random House, Inc. 09 Jun. 2016

Maybe a person cannot recall much about the time spent with their family as a child but may be able to remember some traumatic events in their childhood. Then there are people who have chosen not to deal with the trauma and block all events from their person. In either case, whether they are aware of it or not, the soul makes a record in the blood. Traces and markers of your past trauma that have happened in the tangible have been documented in the intangible soul. These are unseen bondages mastering and governing our actions every day. It is imperative we remind you bondage can be strong/by force or passive/submitted to.

When your soul cries out or speaks up, what is it saying? Who is it calling out to? Have you ever noticed that even though you may desire to be in a particular crowd, you still find yourself in another type of crowd? You may want to be around the righteous and upright, but you seem to draw schemers and manipulators to your person.

A woman may want a righteous man but can only seem to draw men who abuse and handle her without the honor she may feel she deserves. Her soul is crying out; "Abuse!" "Abused!" "Abuses!" If a righteous man's soul would hear, he would give her justice, though when the unrighteous soul hears, he gives her exactly what her soul cries for...Abuse. She then finds herself in another abusive relationship.

The righteous soul and unrighteous soul both hear the same cries of abuse, but they handle them differently. When the unrighteous hears, they take advantage and continue the cycle. This man may have seemed to be all that she was looking for, the whole package, man of her dreams. Though the unseen conversation of souls is establishing a contract of bondage. This is the cycle of tangible trauma affecting our intangible soul.

It's like being set up to fail before you even begin. Therefore, there must be a transformation of soul, not a reformed soul. Your soul does not need to be better, it needs to be purged, so you can stop attracting the very thing destroying you.

Keys to Deliverance: We can take ownership of our souls. We can work out our salvation.[75] Now that we recognize that there is not an evil me and a good me fighting for control, we can now own our transgressions and accept the penalty for walking in the character of the beast.

Have you been struggling in your soul, seeking therapy to try to reform yourself? Are you trying to get a grasp on the chaos inside your being? The lie of tolerance toward the perversion in your soul has not given you peace. Well, I want you to know YHWH did not make a mistake when he made you. The Most High wants you to live defined, refined, and without shame.

You may think that you can cover up the struggle going on inside, but your soul is screaming. In every

---

[75] Philippians 2:12-13

relationship you have had, your soul has aggressively sabotaged your happiness.

Take ownership of that beastly appetite. Ask the Father to help you come into submission to his character. Choose not to live haphazardly but in the perfect order of His design for your life, through His teaching and instructions.

> *If they shall confess their iniquity, and the iniquity of their fathers, with their trespass which they trespassed against me, and that also they have walked contrary unto me; And that I also have walked contrary unto them, and have brought them into the land of their enemies; if then their uncircumcised hearts be humbled, and they then accept of the punishment of their iniquity: Then will I remember my covenant with Jacob, and also my covenant with Isaac, and also my covenant with Abraham will I remember; and I will remember the land.*
> *Leviticus 26:40-42 (KJV)*

Six

THE RECOMPENSE DUE

The climate of the United States of America has continued to denigrate towards a more matriarchal society. Feminism[76] is becoming more and more aggressive. Fear governs our laws. Anyone with an opinion outside of the goal of making everyone *just get along* is vilified. This produces softer men, more postured women, and a generation without any spine. Arguments are no longer considered discussions, they are considered acts of violence. A man with an erect postured spine is no longer manly but a threat.

If that is societies' posture toward standing up, what will be the posture of the righteous? The scriptures demand an upright posture. Isaiah 1:17

---

[76] Feminism – At the root goal is to destroy all patriarchy.

says we need to *seek judgement* and *relieve the oppressed.*

A man is then taught a lie by the hands of his oppressors that he should *turn the other cheek.* As if this was the honorable thing to do. When it only softens him. Did you Y'shua want us to be unassertive without a spine? Hearing people using this text in a perverted way grieves my soul. It advances the patriarchal overthrow and binds a man's soul to be spineless. The wicked slap the righteous then holds them in judgment if they slap back. Even now, as some of you are reading this, you are cringing on the inside due to the fear of taking a stand. People are wronged time and time again, and because of fear of judgment, they never break the cycle. Well sorry, this is not a book about staying in bondage. I'm here to set you free.

What is Recompense?

Recompense is another way saying *reward.*[77] This reward can be good or bad. In the context of the subject matter moving forward, it's reward for the treatment of another person.

Since the case has already established the basis of a soul being a person, can we cause harm to another person without recompense on ourselves?

---

[77] Not trying to make light of all the many complexities of the word, but just so we are not getting into a word study, let's use the simplest form of the word for now.

The universal principle found in Genesis Chapter 9:5-6 says there will be a reward or recompense.

> *I will surely require your blood of your lives. At the hand of every animal I will require it. At the hand of man, even at the hand of every man's brother, I will require the life of man. Whoever sheds man's blood, by man will his blood be shed, for in the image of God made the man.*
> *Genesis 9:5-6 (WEB)*

Y'shua was aware of the principle of recompense. Hence, his statements in Matthew chapter seven when He offers; we should impart our judgments and rebukes from a pure soul, because the same measure we impart to others, will be imparted to us.

> *Judge not, that ye be not judged. For with what judgment ye judge, ye shall be judged: and with what measure ye mete, it shall be measured to you again. And why beholdest thou the mote that is in thy brother's eye, but considerest not the beam that is in thine own eye?*
> *Matthew 7:1-3 (KJV)*

Galatians chapter 6:7 says;

> *Don't be deceived. God is not mocked, for whatever a man sows, that will he also reap.*
> *(WEB)*

Different religions offer different names for the recompense seen universally, but the principle is generally the same. Karma, sowing and reaping, or just getting what you deserve, to name a few. What does recompense have to do with soul bondage? There is a bondage cycle a person can get into by simply not understanding the principles of reward. You can be bound by a wrong done to you or a wrong you have done to another. Without following the principles of the Torah and the Spirit of Messiah to be set free from these cycles, they simply repeat or even increase into greater curses. These curses then can potentially carry on into the next generation. I want to breakdown a couple of these soul binding cycles, rooted in recompense and what principles are offered to break them.

The Offended Soul

> *Then said he unto the disciples, It is **impossible** but that offenses will come: but woe unto him, through whom they come!*
> *Luke 17:1 (KJV)*

An offense is defined as;

> ...*either the cause of anger, displeasure, etc., or a sin. In Scripture we have the special significance of a stumbling-block, or cause of falling, sin, etc.*[78]

The definition offers that an offense can cause a soul to sin, yet Y'shua did not say offenses themselves were sin. Matter of fact, Y'shua in 1 Peter 2:8, is called the rock of offense. Yet offense relates to the cause of a soul to sin or fail, but an offense is not sin. If Y'shua is called the rock of offense, but he does not represent sin, then offenses are not sin.

Y'shua the Master said in Luke 17; it is *impossible* to not get offended. If Y'shua said it was going to be impossible, then I would say, it is impossible. The source validates the point. A soul is going to be offended. The bondage of walking around on egg shells in life, worried about not offending someone, is another way to be bound. It is another opportunity for HaSatan to keep men from posturing themselves and to keep women in abusive situations.

A man walking hunched over, with his head hung low in fear, is where HaSatan wants him to be. Afraid to stand for what is right and not willing to speak to injustice.

A woman being verbally or physically abused yet staying in it because of fear and shame. This is just

---

[78] Offense – International Standard Bible Encyclopedia W. L Walker

the opposite of the spirit of the Torah. He wants the wronged to cry out and not be silent. He wants the men to stand up and walk in an authoritative posture.

Keys to Deliverance: This was the point that Y'shua was offering us. Stop worrying about offending people. Grasp the fact that we are going to offend people, and people are going to offend us, then walk in freedom.

> *Note: In no way am I offering that you intentionally offend a soul. If you live long enough, it is going to happen.*

Maybe you are a man who has not spoken up out of fear of offending a person, so in your silence, you allow injustice or non-sense around you. This is your chance to be set free from the lie of political correctness that has stolen your voice. The Most High wants His people of righteousness to be judges on the earth. The true righteous of Yah corrects injustice and takes an aggressive attitude toward bringing things into order.

If Y'shua said it is impossible to not offend, then he must have had a remedy for all the offended souls being slaughtered, hurt, wounded, and taken by injustice. This is the key. The wisdom is not about the offense you cause, nor the offense that happened to you, but how everyone goes about handling the offense. This will determine whether you walk around in liberty or in bondage to diseases and bitterness. This will determine whether you will have the appropriate soul to set someone else free, because it takes a free soul to set someone else free from injustice.

Offenses, wicked experiences, and injustices that happen to us, in the Hebrew, are a picture of a stained soul[79]. A seed can only produce after its own kind, and the goal of HaSatan is to replicate wickedness. This is how lawlessness is multiplied.[80] Y'shua states; the cycle of wickedness starts with the offense, then leads to betrayal, with the final climax being hatred.

> *And then shall many be offended, and shall betray one another, and shall hate one another.*
> *Matthew 24:10 (KJV)*

The offense, the betrayal, and the hatred, sounds like a good name for a western, but it is a crafty method HaSatan uses to bind souls.

Y'shua said first comes the offense, then the betrayal, then the hatred. This is illustrated in the process flow chart below.

---

[79] "Wicked" - An action that causes a stain of immorality. H#5765, #5766, #5767
[80] Matthew 24:12 - Because iniquity will be multiplied, the love of many will grow cold.

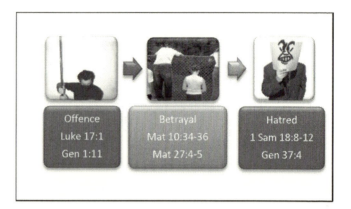

Paul offered we can be angry but not sin.[81] Can we then be offended and not sin as well? Since offenses are the cause of anger. The principle to prevent ourselves from being bound is to handle the offense at the light phase, versus trying to handle it at the heavy phase.

This is a hermeneutic principle called Kal va-chomer[82]. It means *light and heavy or the greater principle*. When Y'shua was saying in Matthew 5:29 to cast away members of your body because of the offense they cause, he was using the principle called Kal va-chomer.

---

[81] Angry sin not – Ephesians 4:26
[82] Hermeneutics – Encyclopedia of Judaism -Geoffrey Wigoder 1989 Publishing edition

> *And if thy right eye offend thee, pluck it out, and cast it from thee: for it is profitable for thee that one of thy members should perish, and not that thy whole body should be cast into hell.*
> *Matthew 5:29 (KJV)*

The offense will come, but before it gets to the betrayal phase and the hatred phase, a transition needs to happen. The principles of the Torah apply naturally and spiritually. The principle I use as a reference when it comes to handling offenses is Deuteronomy 22:23-24. This is where Moshe[83] offers;

> *If a damsel that is a virgin be betrothed unto an husband, and a man find her in the city, and lie with her; Then ye shall bring them both out unto the gate of that city, and ye shall stone them with stones that they die; the damsel, because she cried not, being in the city; and the man, because he hath humbled his neighbour's wife: so thou shalt put away evil from among you. (KJV)*

Moshe shows us a type of soul that has the potential to get help but chooses not to cry out for it. Because of this refusal to do so in return, their penalty is death. Why death? The silence the soul

---

[83] Moshe – Moses common transliteration meaning drawn out

chooses when there was help available is seen as rejection to help. Why would someone reject help? There are too many variables to offer, but the question in context of what you are reading about needs to be; *Why do we not cry out when there is available help at the point of offense?*

The most tactical action to take when offenses comes is to transition from the realm of death that HaSatan is making as a trap. Crying out, as in the principle of vows and oaths[84], is the honest, humble, and most trusting option for a soul. Before the carnal mind tries to complicate this principle, and to keep the revelation and the effective application from taking root, let's look at a simple story in Genesis.

Peshat: There were twin brothers named Jacob and Esau that rivaled with each other even while still in the womb of the mother.[85] In the climax of their rivalry, Jacob found himself at a point of decision. The Most High was commanding him to return to the land, but his brother who was an offended soul stood at the entrance. This became an offense to Jacob.[86] Jacob in return cries out;

---

[84] Will be discussed more in depth in the next chapter.
[85] Genesis 25:22-23
[86] Genesis 32:9-12

> *Deliver me, I pray thee, from the hand of my brother, from the hand of Esau: for I fear him, lest he will come and smite me, and the mother with the children. And thou saidst, I will surely do thee good, and make thy seed as the sand of the sea, which cannot be numbered for multitude.*
> *Gen. 32:11-12 (KJV)*

Drash: The transparency of Jacob was to cry out to the Most High with honesty. Yes, the Most High knew he was afraid, but Jacob had to cry out. The trap of HaSatan is to get a soul not to cry out, to stay quiet. When a soul says to themselves; *Yah, knows my pain, my captivity, my fears, my situation, I don't need to cry out.* This is the point when HaSatan has won.

Remez: Once again, the principle was because there was help and the soul did not cry out, the penalty shall be death. The Father of all souls wants to be our deliverer and salvation, and HaSatan wants us to keep our mouths shut and remain in bondage.

When there is a violation that causes an offense, the principle requires for us to cry out. Immediately speak up, why let it maturate?

> *Yahweh said, "I have surely seen the affliction of my people who are in Egypt, and **have heard their cry** because of their taskmasters, for I know their sorrows. I have come down to deliver them out of the hand of the Egyptians, and to bring them up out of that land to a good and large land, to a land flowing with milk and honey; to the place of the Canaanite, the Hittite, the Amorite, the Perizzite, the Hivite, and the Jebusite.*
> *Exodus 3:7-8 (WEB)*

> *I will go down now, and see whether they have done altogether according **to the cry of it**, which is come to me. If not, I will know."*
> *Genesis 18:21 (WEB)*

Principles in Action: The freedom is in the details, those honest details. Jacob said; *I am afraid*. Express the obvious, the hidden, the feeling, even express what is not understood. If your soul is confused, express it. If your soul is angry, express it. If your soul is just frustrated, express it to the father as David did in Psalms so many times.

A Remedy for the Offended Soul

> *Ye have heard that it hath been said, an eye for an eye, and a tooth for a tooth: But I (Y'shua) say unto you, that ye resist not evil: but whosoever shall smite thee on thy right cheek, turn to him the other also.*
> *Matthew 5:38-39 (KJV)*

Peshat: Automatically, when reading Matthew 5:38-39, your mind may take you to the picture of a man being bullied or slapped into submission by another man. The taste of mercy and weakness may linger on your pallet. Yet, let us not forget, Y'shua was a Torah observant Hebrew. He understood the principles and the need to make the spirit of the principles stand up.

Scriptures like these have given congregations power over men. Such hierarchies men submit to are abusive. They take advantage of men knowing they are not prepared for the level of deception coming from their position, power, and influence.

Remez: The verse needs to be examined to understand the deeper meaning of the text. Starting at Matthew 5:38, Y'shua starts with a remez to the Torah, in the section of scripture that Hebrews known as *Mishpatim,* judgments.

> *If men strive, and hurt a woman with child, so that her fruit depart from her, and yet no mischief follow: he shall be surely punished, according as the woman's husband will lay upon him; and he shall pay as the judges determine. And if any mischief follow, then thou shalt give life for life, Eye for eye, tooth for tooth, hand for hand, foot for foot, Burning for burning, wound for wound, stripe for stripe.*
> *Exodus 21:22-25 (KJV)*

Right away, the text offers a contradiction to the whole idea of a weak-postured man that is turning the other cheek in submission.

"*If men strive...*" here we have two men striving, but without the Torah addressing the strife. It does bring to attention that there may be an innocent bystander who may be harmed in the altercation, more specifically, a woman with child. The Torah shows us the most innocent of bystanders, a woman and her unborn. The Torah's position on woman being protected by men is of the highest priority. Then, when we add an unborn innocent baby to the dynamic, it becomes the perfect innocent bystander scenario.

Why does the Torah not offer a rebuke for striving, when Y'shua said we should turn the other cheek and love our neighbor? You can still love your neighbor when there is an altercation. Men are built in a way that allows them to have the ability to physically fight to resolve disputes or offer physical correction to a brother in love.

When I have had opportunities to teach men that the scriptures are not against men fighting, the shock they have is amazing. The soft-palleted, matriarchal, happy hippie Jesus has permeated their thought life so deeply, they have become bound to a weak spirit. Castrated before even having a chance to fight or stand up for themselves or their families.

Here is a good example of; *first comes the natural then the spirit*. If a man is castrated on earth because he has been told to be passive, then how will he be a spiritual warrior in the heavenlies. Is this why women are raising up prayer warrior groups, while men are trying to understand their *He-Motions*[87]? So, if the Torah is not against men fighting, what is the point of Y'shua's saying; ...*turn the other cheek*?

Exodus continues to say after we see men striving;

> *...hurt a woman with child, so that her fruit depart from her, and yet no mischief follow: ...*

Drash: The woman who was supposed to be protected is now *hurt*, this is a violation, what needs to happen? The Torah says; this needs to be made

---

[87] *He-Motions* – T.D. Jakes' book where encourages men to delve into the emotional and spiritual aspects of themselves.

right with the husband. This is offered two-fold. One by what the husband says is compensation, and two by what the judge says is lawful compensation.

These laws of retaliation were a necessary principle needed to make sure the offended party comes to a place of healing and justice. These judgments were not supposed to be a punishment, but an opportunity to make things right, *justice*. When we look at the judgments of the Torah and try to make them law and not deliverance, this is when they can become an offense to us. This judgment was designed to deliver the hurt soul of the husband. If someone has the right heart and honors righteousness, they should want to see his healing. If the heart is stony or bitter, they will only see law. Like a selfish spoiled child being told to do something they do not want to do. The child is going to be offended, throw a temper tantrum, then rebel.

The husband of the hurt woman now has the right to say what he would need to make restitution for his loss. What will it take to bring peace to a wounded soul? When the bitterness within is needing to come to a place of resolve and healing? What is the necessary recompense? The laws of retaliation were only going to be able to offer healing to a certain degree. Y'shua knew this. He then places the burden on the offender *NOT* the offended. Y'shua states;

> *that ye resist not evil: but whosoever shall smite thee on thy right cheek, turn to him the other also.*

Sud: He offers a principle of deliverance for any potentially bound soul, by stating, *go the extra mile*. Most theologians think that just because the text begins by saying; *resist not evil,* Y'shua is referring to the victim. The implication becomes, if you are being abused, submit to the abuse. If you are being robbed give him the keys to your car as well as your wallet. *No*. A resounding *no*.

Pastors are going to seminaries and biblical schools to learn this errant way of thinking. Stephen L. Harris and his colleagues of writers and theologians make a suggestion in their book *Understanding the Bible,* a book that is a part of the common curriculum used in colleges. He writes;

> *Jesus goes beyond its literal application to demand that his listeners give up their traditional right to retaliate in kind. Is Jesus, then, urging people to submit passively to those who wrong them?*[88]

I will answer your rhetorical question with a huge *no*. Y'shua was not speaking to the victims, telling them to submit to their abusers. The *evil* he is referring to is the judgment the husband said would be necessary for his family to come to a place of deliverance and healing. The *evil* he is referring to is

---

[88] Understanding the Bible by Stephen L Harris – Page 386

the judgment given by the judge designed to bring restitution.

It is very common in the Hebrew text to see the word *evil* used in the context to mean judgment. Example; the Most High says;

> *If that nation, against whom I have pronounced, turn from their evil,* ***I will repent of the evil*** *that I thought to do unto them.*
> *Jeremiah 18:8 (KJV)*

> *Now therefore go to, speak to the men of Judah, and to the inhabitants of Jerusalem, saying, Thus saith the LORD; Behold,* ***I frame evil against you****, and devise a device against you: return ye now every one from his evil way, and make your ways and your doings good.*
> *Jeremiah 18:11 (KJV)*

The Most High refers to the judgment He was about to pass down to Israel as *evil*. This does not make Him the evil person, nor will it make another person evil if they are simply offering someone the recompense due.

Y'shua was trying to get us to see the need for there to be a healing. The victims needed a judgement or else, without that offense finding justice, their soul could be bound, which will ultimately lead to more diseases and death.

Example: Bob and Jack got into a physical altercation. A wild punch from Jack, which was intended for Bob's stomach, landed in the stomach of pregnant Jane passing by. Tom hears of the accident that caused harm to his innocent wife Jane and unborn child. Tom now has an offense and a need to be delivered through restitution, not just retaliation.

Retaliation only allows Tom to somewhat be compensated for his loss, measure for measure. This is the challenge Y'shua offers us. Jack is in the wrong, Tom and the judge will be offering Jack steps he can take to make it right with Tom and his family.

Tom tells the court the *evil* (judgment) that can bring him to a place of healing is striking Jack on the cheek for the wrong he caused his family. The court also offers a judgment of 50 shekels of silver. This is where Y'shua steps in on the story and says to Jack;

> *Okay, you know you wronged Tom, and he's coming over to strike you on the cheek for his healing. Now, when he does strike you on the one cheek, turn the other cheek. This way, you both can positively know you have gone the extra mile for his deliverance.*

Principles in Action: The principle is so loud throughout the scriptures. What are you willing to do to deliver that bound, offended soul? The demand Y'shua is offering is *not* to be passive to our abusers, but to be aggressively humble toward the ones we have wronged so they can be delivered. He calls for them to be free from the bondage that keeps their soul from healing.

Under the passive Christian concept, Jack should now be able to kick Tom's wife again when she gets pregnant a second time. Which is flat out wrong!!

Keys to Deliverance: You have offended someone. Whether you recognize it or not. This makes you an *offender* of souls. The remedy for the offended soul is to be aggressively delivered by the offender. Ask the Father to reveal to you the offended souls you have offended in need of your deliverance. Go to them, throwing yourself down at their mercy. Ask them what you could do to make things right. Then go the extra mile above their request. This will unlock an area of blessings for you and them.

Jacob, the offender, had Esau at a place of offense for 20 years. Esau was bound by the offense of his brother with no relief. Jacob then goes to him in humility, showering him with gifts. He was willing to give him more than just the one cheek so that Esau could come to a place of healing.

If Jacob did not come to the humility necessary to allow Esau to heal, he may have never been able to go into the land. Esau represents all the offended souls that stand in front of the promised land, or more specifically, our personal promise land. What will you be willing to do to make sure that those souls you have offended come to a place of healing?

Stand up! Your abuser does not get to slap you twice. Your abuser does not get another stab at you. <u>The remedy for the offended soul is to stop believing the lie that you should lay down passively and give more opportunity to the abuser who is harming you.</u> If you are truly the victim, stand up and cry out for justice. Cause the righteous ones to be held accountable. Demand justice, from your judges, leaders, and responsible parties for your soul. Recompense is the reward every person deserves, good or evil, so a soul will not remain bound.

A Soul that is Stained

> *Follow peace with all men, and holiness, without which no man shall see the Lord: Looking diligently lest any man fail of the grace of God; lest any root of bitterness springing up trouble you, and thereby many be defiled;*
> *Hebrews 12:14-15 (KJV)*

I can recall the very first gangster rap album that I heard. At the risk of exposing my age, this was when gangster rap first came out. The idea of parental advisory labels had not even been considered until this style of music was released. My cousins and siblings were Jr. High School and High School teenagers, while I was still in the fifth grade. Today, that style of music is heard in some homes from birth. Since I was growing up in a religious home where gospel and some mild rock was tolerated, you can imagine my shock. The language and depravity opened my imagination like Eve biting from the forbidden fruit. For me, it gave me a sense of maturity over my peers. While with the teenagers, who HaSatan geared the music toward, it empowered their sense of rebellion. Not quite yet a teenager at the time to fully grasp hold of the rebellion, but as I became older, I got it.

Each generation has a rebellious music that stamps their era, so most people understand. As a teenager, you just like it because of the beat, so they say. What is really happening in the spirit realm is principle. HaSatan uses agents who are bitter toward the hurt and offense caused to them to reproduce the same fruit. This unsuspecting teenager who is hormonal and misunderstood, they connect with the hurt. In their submission of will, they become defiled.

My defiled soul produced in me a mis-treatment of women, disrespect toward my elders, and a contempt toward wisdom. I was a typical teenager, bitter and mad at the world because I couldn't measure up to its unrealistic expectations. I was carnal and did not know, it was all fake. That bitterness in any of us is fertile ground for HaSatan's seed. The artist who created the music was bitter, I submitted to it, then in return, it defiled my soul. I then became an agent of HaSatan, out to defile other souls.

The author of Hebrews challenges us with the thought that we can *fail grace*[89], and in return, the bitterness that is buried within causes others to be defiled. We mentioned the stained soul, but how does a person get a stain on their soul? The stained soul is a bitter offended soul.

At the root of wickedness is an offense, that wickedness is the stain on your soul, since the offense was not handled at the light stage, it springs up as a fruit for others to partake. This wicked fruit defiles the soul of the person who consumes it, which Hebrews 12 shows us. See illustration chart below:

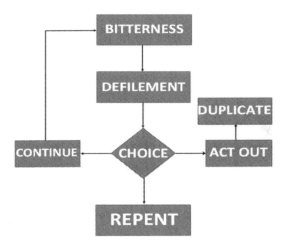

---

[89] *Fail* or *fall from grace*. The Hebrew concept of grace is only as effective as the permission we give grace in our lives. Since His grace/Spirit is sufficient, when we do not yield to His grace we fail grace, not *fall from grace*. Fail, because we don't respond to grace.

The illustration shows that first bitterness sets in. Bitterness is at the root of many of our illnesses. After bitterness goes unchecked, the soul becomes defiled with the goal of reproducing the same defilement in others. At some point, you have the choice to continue the cycle, repent, or the worst of the three, act out your defilement.

This is another cycle that can have a soul bound for years. There are souls in position all around us, within proximity just to defile us. Under the right circumstance and the right climate, their fruit springs up waiting for us to partake.

Example: TMZ is a global gossip television and internet media celebrity tabloid. TMZ is a representation of the wickedness of the defiled soul out to defile others. When TMZ asks their questions to their victims, because they are a gossip tabloid, their interest is not *How are you doing? No.* They want the juicy slander that will get them more views, clicks, and attention.

Each question is intended to insight, instigate, agitate, stir up or cause drama or backlash. They are the intentional wickedness trying to defile the souls of the interviewer, the reader, the listener, and viewer.

If we could be wise enough to recognize this wicked agenda to defile a soul, how much more effective would we be at issuing rebukes or not participating? TMZ has come under criticism because of their choice to exploit, slander, denigrate, agitate, instigate, antagonize, and demonize individuals leading to destructive behavior, depression, suicide attempts, and some cases, successful suicides.

Though TMZ is just an example of the type of spirit that lurks to defile your soul, even worse destroy your soul, there are people in your social circles with the same agenda.

If HaSatan can get a person to partake in the defiled fruit of bitterness, leading them to act out or even continue the cycle, it will be another one bound for him.

Keys to Deliverance: In this defiled world, defilement is available for any of us at any time. Have you been a victim of defilement? Have you consciously submitted your soul to the bitterness of your peer's poison? Ungodly hatred towards individuals who you don't even know. Have you had the opportunity to escape, but chose to not submit to His Spirit causing you to fail grace?

His grace is still here, willing to empower you toward His righteousness and order. It is time to stop acting out your defilement and come to repentance. Allow the Spirit of the Most High to purge you of all uncleanness.

i. Ask him to reveal to you the day your defilement began.
ii. Curse the day you submitted to your defilement and ask for forgiveness.
iii. Give your bitterness to Him. Relinquish the attachments to hate and self.

iv. Then as the Spirit, not your religious mind[90,] gives you revelation on where you need to offer recompense, do so.

Recompense is continuous. The acts of love toward our neighbors will be a process we will go through until He returns. We will continue to offend others and fall into the traps of defilement. The principles of deliverance will continually need to be applied. The other option is to remain in a perverted soul state and continue to act out your defilement and live in lack. Today is your day to turn it all around.

---

[90] Religious mind – This is not a twelve-step program. Remember, any attempt to act with an un-pure soul will only defile a soul. You must be led by His Spirit at the pace He chooses.

Seven

THE LEGALITIES OF SOUL BONDAGE

E nvision a person being held captive illegally but has no knowledge of their rights to be set free. In the spiritual warfare we are faced with every day, the necessity to know our rights in the Most High is imperative. Knowing our rights allows us to fight effectively against the armies of darkness. We can then handle ourselves with precision within the parameters of the battle grounds and could exercise liberties when bound lawfully or unlawfully.

What if HaSatan went outside of the parameter's set by the Most High, when He gave him permission to test Job[91] the first time? HaSatan was not allowed

---

[91] Book of Job found in the cannon of scriptures

to touch Job's person the first time; but what if, in this example, he began to do so? This would have been a violation of the boundaries the Most High set for HaSatan. Today, still, there are boundaries in our lives HaSatan must remain within. Just as HaSatan has boundaries, the Most High's people have rights found in the Torah. When we are unaware of our rights, we become silent in the face of injustice versus crying out when the violation occurs.

It is difficult to get others to understand that just because we exist in the tangible here and now, it does not mean there is not an intangible world existing all around us. Just as the tangible world has laws and boundaries, so does the intangible world. Let's present it like this:

The job of the Federal Communications Commission (FCC) in the United States, is to control or direct by a rule, principle, method, or standard, the "airwaves." These are the same principles HaSatan uses when it comes to the spiritual sovereignties. He is the *"prince of the powers"*[92] governing the air.

The FCC is able to accomplish their rule by establishing laws on the tangible earth through written documents to oversee how people can govern themselves in the intangible air. The tangible laws written on earth by the FCC govern the intangible air. The parallel is how the Torah is written on the earth, which then governs the intangible. It is our

---

[92] Ephesians 2:2

application of laws that permits or does not permit HaSatan to carry out his purpose in our lives.

How does the FCC know if the tangible laws have been violated? They monitor the airwaves and listen to the complaints of others who feel they have had their rights violated. They report these violations to established bureaus, who regulate their policies and penalties for breaking the established law. This is the same with the Torah. We are commanded to establish judges and officers to receive these complaints of violations of laws within all of our gates. The judges and officers were commanded to meet a certain criterion. The Exodus 18:21 says;

> *Moreover you shall provide out of all the people able men, such as fear God: men of truth, hating unjust gain; and place such over them, to be rulers of thousands, rulers of hundreds, rulers of fifties, and rulers of tens. (WEB)*

HaSatan and his fallen ones have been aware of this system for millennia. They are subject to the Torah and our rights. As a matter of fact, we are willing to go as far as to say they are master legalists. If we would truly grasp the magnitude of this, we would not be trying to fight a master attorney with no legal knowledge. Paul puts it another way when he states:

> *For we wrestle not against flesh and blood, but against principalities, against powers, against the rulers of the darkness of this world, against spiritual wickedness in high places.*
> *Ephesians 6:12 (KJV)*
>
> *Wherein in time past ye walked according to the course of this world, according to the prince of the **power of the air**, the spirit that now worketh in the children of disobedience:*
> *Ephesians 2:2 (KJV)*

Just as the FCC establishes laws for governing the air. The Torah also offers laws and rights that must be abided by in the air/intangible. Abandoning the Torah is abandoning the rights to have ministry within the air/intangible. It's like abandoning the ability to fight the powers on their turf. Y'shua stated, *until* there is a shaking of the powers in the heavens, He will not return (paraphrased).[93]

The battle HaSatan has been waging on the earth is a battle he has been bringing to us; but Y'shua expects us to take the battle to him. From the writings of Paul, it seems this was his expectation as well.

There is a universal law that gives people, being violated, rights within the Torah. Due to the abandoning of the Torah, we have lost our voice to

---

[93] Mark 13:24-37; Matthew 24:39

complain to the powers in the air; the Most High, or about the powers of the air; HaSatan. Hosea 4:6 says;

> *My people are destroyed for lack of knowledge: because thou hast rejected knowledge, I will also reject thee, that thou shalt be no priest to me: seeing thou hast forgotten the law of thy God, I will also forget thy children. (KJV)*

Paraphrasing this for better understanding, Hosea is saying; because the people of the Most High have forgotten their rights in the Torah, they and their children will not have a voice to speak up against the iniquity[94] that will come as a result. We come to this paraphrase by looking at the word "Destroy." In this usage, "destroy" means "to become silent like one that is dead." In addition, *"Destroy"* has another meaning, which is *"likeness, a son from the blood of his father resembles his father."*[95]

Taking the interpretation of this word into context with the following verses and the rest of the chapter, the offered paraphrase gives an accurate explanation that each generation is becoming more and more silenced. One generation after another loses their voice, rights, and ability to fight against their captors.

---

[94] Iniquity – Sins passed down from the father, gross injustice.
[95] "Likeness, Destroy" – damah #H1820, #H1821 #H1819 and AHL

Going over the legalities of bondage is not to bring people under legalism; it is to bring people into freedom. There is a law at work whether we want to recognize it or not, and it is not just destroying us, but is also destroying the future generations.

> *Note: The principles here are in no priority of greater or lesser arrangement.*

Christ Ordained Authority

> *Most assuredly I tell you, whatever things you will bind on earth will be bound in heaven, and whatever things you will release on earth will be released in heaven.*
> *Matthew 18:18 (WEB)*

This is a popular verse used by charismatic Christianity to claim their ability to bind up "Satan" and his host. Yet in the Torah, from a Hebraic perspective, this scripture has an idiom meaning; "whatever you permit, allowed in the Torah, and whatever you do not permit, disallow according to the Torah."

Y'shua is speaking to Peter on one occasion[96], then to his disciples on the other occasion when this idiom is used. In its simplest form, *whatever things you will bind on earth will be bound in heaven* speaks plainly, but what does the *bind* and *bound* mean? How can someone "not permit" on earth, and then the counter reaction becomes that it is not permitted in heaven or in the intangible?

When Y'shua was speaking to Peter, he was giving him the authority to govern the assemblies by offering righteous rulings and judgments that were legally binding. He was selected to be an emissary or ambassador for the ekklesia[97]. Peter was elected by Christ to have the authority to operate in this capacity. His wisdom and anointing given to him, by Christ, gave him the authority to "permit" or "not permit" certain actions to take place in the assembly. His words were "binding."

---

[96] Matthew 16:19

[97] The conscience decision to use the Greek word "ekklesia" versus, the most commonly mistranslated used word, "church" was so to help offer an interpretation that points to "a called-out congregation or assembly" and not a building.

> *Bind; as a legal phrase indicates an agreement has been consciously made, and certain actions are now either required or prohibited.[98] Binding is a legal relation that remains in force and virtue, and continues to impose duties or obligations, it is said to be "binding." A man is bound by his contract or promise, by a judgment or decree against him, by his bond or a covenant.[99]*

When Y'shua stated to Peter he could *bind and lose*, he was using a legal term understandable in the legal system of the Torah. Peter was given binding authority. Does this mean we all were given binding authority in the congregation? Certainly not, this would be chaos in the assembly. The usage of *binding* and *losing* has been greatly misinterpreted by the *Charismatic Christian Church*. The "keys" to the Kingdom means spiritual authority[100], not some doorman standing at the pearly gates. Speaking threats to HaSatan to bind him is completely futile. The misconception that you have been given authority over HaSatan has been a perpetuated lie. You may expect victory, but only through Christ, the author and finisher. Even Michael the archangel, one

---

[98] A Law Dictionary, By John Bouvier. Published 1856.
[99] Black's Law Dictionary Free 2nd Ed. and The Law Dictionary
[100] "Key" - Based on the Random House Dictionary, © Random House, Inc.

of the most powerful of the angels, did not rebuke HaSatan, but said;

> "...*May the Lord rebuke you!*"
> *Jude 1:9 (WEB)*

Torah Ordained Authority

Lucy went to the deliverance camp meeting seeking deliverance from a debt she vowed to pay. The debt was too much for her and had become overwhelming. It became a burden on her life and kept her bound from functioning and flowing in the Messiah. It was a distraction to her spiritual growth.

Pop Quiz: How do we deliver Lucy's soul?
Do we   a: Pray for her deliverance
              b: Decree and declare her free
              c: Ask her, where is her husband
              d: Believe God, for peace

Answer: Keep reading

In Numbers chapter 30, it states; *vows* and *oaths* can legally *bind* a soul.

> *When a man vows **a vow** to Yahweh, or swears **an oath to bind his soul** with a bond, he shall not break his word; he shall do according to all that proceeds out of his mouth....*
> *Numbers 30:2 (WEB)*

A vow is when promises are made to perform an act if another performs a certain act[101]. However, when a person offers an oath, they are putting on a yoke, a binding agreement including the curse for violating the oath[102].

Vows and oaths carry the connotation that promises spoken are weighty and valuable in the legal parameters of the Torah. If Y'shua shows us in Matthew 12:36-37 the attitude taken towards *idle* words on the day of judgment, how much more weight do words spoken in the spirit of promise have?

> *"I tell you that every idle word that men speak, they will give account of it in the day of judgment. For by your words you will be justified, and by your words you will be condemned."*
> *Matthew 12:36-37 (WEB)*

---

[101] "Vow" Hebrews Strong's #H2385
[102] "Oath" –Hebrews Strong's # 7621 and 423

This would be a good time to bring your attention to the language in the Torah that authorizes these promises to bind your soul.

If vows and oaths are what bind you, then who or what has the authority to loosen you? This is where authority comes in; according to Numbers chapter 30, only a specific authority can unbind certain bound souls. So, just because a person has a microphone and some buzz words like "decree" and "declare," it does not mean they have the authority to break that soul's bondage.

The Torah is very specific about who has the authority to loosen certain legally bound souls. It states; ***true deliverance is between a man and his wife, between a father and his daughter, being in her youth, in her father's house.***[103] The true deliverance ministry starts in the home and ends in the home. It is possible to attend 100 camp meetings and tent revivals for deliverance, but remain bound, due to the ignorance we have towards the Torah's legal standards.

Numbers 30 Breakdown

For a better understanding, I want to ensure that you have a good grasp of the Torah principles established in Numbers 30. I have included extensive detailed charts of the breakdown. Going forward without comprehension to the principles presented

---

[103] Numbers 30:16

here, may lead to a misunderstanding to the collective principle.

Numbers 30:2, in relationship to the male species, really lays it out plainly. Whenever a man vows or binds his soul with an oath, he shall do according to all that proceeds out of his mouth. There is no a legal precedent presented that excuses the man from his bond. At no point in the chapter, does the Most High state an outside intercessor can step in and annul the words proceeded from his mouth. A man's words are binding to YHWH (reference illustration 1).

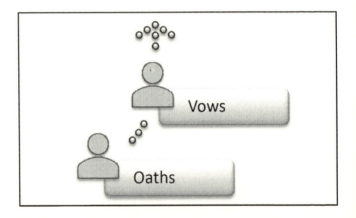

Numbers 30:3-5 in relationship to the females that are *in her father's house, in her youth,* the Torah is not silent on how she is to be handled when it comes to her vows and oaths.

> *Also when a woman vows a vow to Yahweh, and binds herself by a bond, being in her father's house, in her youth, and her father hears her vow, and her bond with which she has bound her soul, and her father holds his peace at her; then all her vows shall stand, and every bond with which she has bound her soul shall stand. But if her father disallow her in the day that he hears, none of her vows, or of her bonds with which she has bound her soul, shall stand: and Yahweh will forgive her, because her father disallowed her.*
> *Numbers 30:3-5 (WEB)*

Following the verses as they are illustrated in the flowchart below. Keep in mind the chart starts at the bottom then reads up.

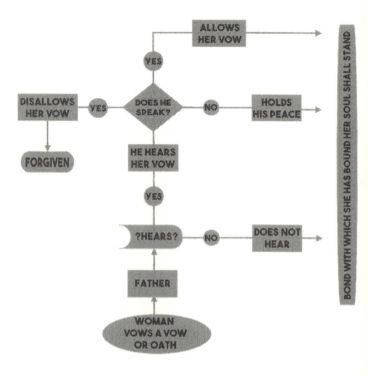

Breaking down the chart into more detail, I have chosen to use snap shots of each section.

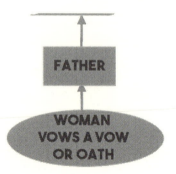

1 The first distinction that must be noticed is the text specifically says vows and oaths *only*. This is a young woman in her father's house as shown.

2 The Torah then addresses that the father heard this vow or oath. This is not a decision point, but it can be arbitrary or even happenstance. Meaning, maybe he did not have the intention to hear, but so happened to have overheard. Either way, the father has heard the woman speak this vow or oath.

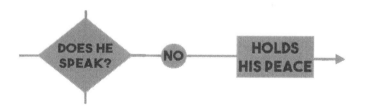

3 Next, the Torah asks if the father holds his peace. This would be a decision point for the father. He has chosen to hold his peace for whatever reason. Which

the Torah considers to be acceptance to the words she has spoken. In return, she becomes legally bound.

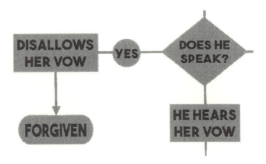

4 Numbers 30:5 begins by saying; if the decision of the father is to disallow what he has heard, then YHWH will forgive because of the father has disallowed. The authority of the father over his daughter cancels the vow or oath that he has heard and has chosen to disallow it.

I have taken the liberty to illustrate the other two possible options that aren't so plainly written.

Option 1: If the father does not hear the vow or oath spoken by the woman, then the vow or oath stands. Illustrated in snap shot 5.

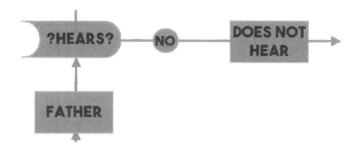

Option 2: If the father does hear, then he chooses to agree or affirm her vow and oaths. These too will stand and will legally bind her soul. Illustrated in snapshot 6.

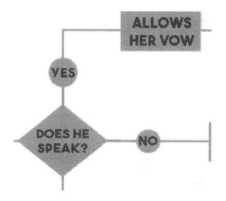

Hopefully, through those rundowns, you have a better understanding of the laws concerning a young woman that may still be under her father's house/covering. It would be necessary to mention that *young* may point to age, but according to the Torah, there is no such thing as a headless woman. A woman would go from the mastery of her father to the mastery of her husband, always ensuring she is protected. I will talk about those legal parameters in detail soon.

When it comes to the husband in Numbers 30, the dynamic changes drastically.

> *If she be married to a husband, while her vows are on her, or the rash utterance of her lips, with which she has bound her soul, and her husband hear it, and hold his peace at her in the day that he hears it; then her vows shall stand, and her bonds with which she has bound her soul shall stand. But if her husband disallow her in the day that he hears it, then he shall make void her vow which is on her, and the rash utterance of her lips, with which she has bound her soul: and Yahweh will forgive her.*
> *Numbers 30:6-8 (WEB)*

Here I use the same chart but add one essential change, making the husband the true cultivator of his wife's soul. See chart below.

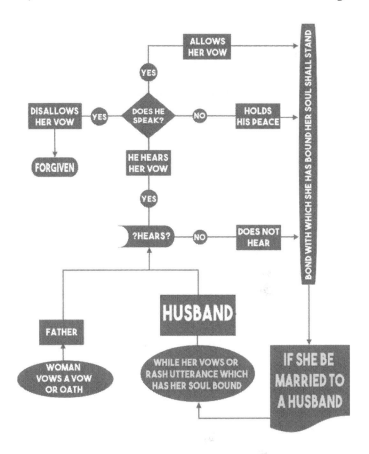

... he shall make void her vow which is on her, and the rash utterance of her lips... The Torah is offering the right of protection to the woman to the highest extent. Her protection even goes to the point that the words which could potentially be damaging to her soul can be cancelled by her husband. Unlike the father, the husband's ability to annul her words is greater. Where the father was only able to disallow vows and oaths, the husband takes on the ability to

disallow even rash utterances. The magnitude of this is enormous!! The husband can now annul the vows and oaths the father may have established, and *the rash words spoken outside of wisdom, usually in the form of a vow*[104].

What about the things spoken in anger her father was not privy to hearing? The husband becomes the true husbandman of the ground and tills the garden. He works the land of his wife to discover these utterances with the ultimate goal of cancelling all that is necessary and setting her soul free.

A husbandman is defined as; *the servant, steward and cultivator of land*. When we see the woman as the garden and the man as the husbandman, we can then see the beautiful system the Most High intended.

The man and woman submit to each other as Paul said in Ephesians 5:21:

> *Submitting yourselves one to another in the fear of God.*

The woman submits to the husband by sharing those areas of her life that need his cultivation. She submits to him the pains and areas of bondage that have kept her bound in her soul, causing her to not be able to reproduce as she was created to do. The

---

[104] "Utter" - Hebrews Strong's #4008 and 981 - Ancient Hebrew Lexicon of the Bible

husband, in return, submits himself as servant to the land and works it. He painstakingly works by the sweat of his brow to get to the root of every thorn and thistle; disallowing HaSatan the dominion over those areas of his garden. Taking back the dominion of his property and showing himself as a good steward and in return enjoys the fruit of his labor.

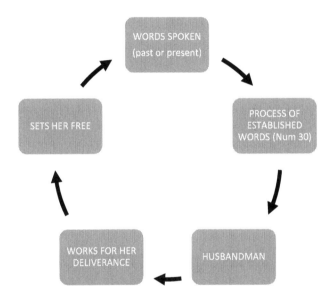

This is the cycle of a husband being constantly in the state of husbandman. Though the process for hearing and disallowing is the same as the father, there is a section of the chart that cycles.

Words are spoken, whether they are rash utterances or conscience vows and oaths. They go through the process of being established according to Numbers 30. The husbandman then, in turn, could work for his wife's deliverance or allow her to remain bound. When he chooses to work for her deliverance and set her free, the cycle continues with new words old words etc.

The cycle continues until the husband dies or divorces. The Torah then adds; if there are still areas of the woman's life, now widowed or divorced, she did not submit to her husband for release, then she will remain bound. The words she is bound by that were not dealt with by the husband, for whatever reason, she will remain bound to them. Her opportunity to be set free while he was alive or married to her has now been lost.

> *But every vow of a widow, and of her that is divorced, wherewith they have bound their souls, shall stand against her. And if she vowed in her husband's house or bound her soul by a bond with an oath; And her husband heard it, and held his peace at her, and disallowed her not: then all her vows shall stand, and every bond wherewith she bound her soul shall stand.*
> *Numbers 30:9-11 (KJV)*

Order of the Husband and Wife

Bob and Lucy decided to get married. Bob, just like as he would purchase land from any other person, purchases the deed of ownership from Lucy's father. This marriage contract or deed of purchase he holds secures him as land owner, and the woman represents the land. What place or right does a stranger passing by have in telling Bob what to do with his land?[105]

Numbers 30 shows the responsibility and authority of Bob as the owner of the land. Bob is the husbandman over his land. When Bob and Lucy have a daughter, Bob then has the same responsibility and authority over her. The land is the women of his household still under his authority.

Bob is not just a flunky that is supposed to bring home the money for the woman to shop and pay bills. He is also the authority over the family's souls. Whether they are submitted or un-submitted, Bob is the ranking authority to loosen their bondage. Even if Bob doesn't know his authority, and the woman seeks another means to be loosened, she is still legally bound unless the husbandman lawfully unbinds her.

With a better understanding of the natural principal of how we are bound and loosened on earth, let us re-examine Y'shua's principle. Y'shua states *if you are bound on earth, you are bound in the heavenlies.*

The Most High honors the legal precedent already established in His Torah. Not every person who tries to rescue a princess is her knight in shining armor. Before we attempt to slay the dragon in the

---

[105] Woman as land seen in scripture – Jeremiah 3:8-9

intangible, we should consider that to even approach may be unauthorized. A poor helpless princess could be under the authority of a husbandman she may not have disclosed or could not be aware of. Unaware of the law, she could have submitted her land, spiritually and physically. Subsequently, the attempts to spoil her land can only happen if the strongman is bound first.[106]

Another example of *if you are bound on earth, you are bound in the heavenlies* could be as simple as understanding our earthly soul's bondage can influence our ability to fight in the heavenlies. If we are bound in our homes (earth), then we are bound in the heavenlies. The ability to fight in the heavenlies is handicapped when you are not aware of the authority or ranking to fight. Maybe we thought we didn't measure up in our ability to fight, when the whole time, it could've been that we may not have had the authority to fight.

How Do I Know If I Have Authority (woman)?

> *But I would have you know that the head of every man is Christ, and the head of the woman is the man, and the head of Christ is God.*
> *1 Corinthians 11:3 (World English Bible)*

---

[106] Strong man reference – Parable in Matthew 12 starting at 22-37

From the scripture above, you can see the authority is given to the head. The head of woman is the *man species*. Before the urge to stop reading overtakes you, I would like to suggest you do not let your carnal mind confuse your understanding by substituting "authority" with "right." Instead, look at the authority of man over woman as a right a woman has. Women have the right to have a provider, protector, visionary, cultivator, hunter, husbandman, master, and intercessor for their soul. There should not be any headless woman[107] in the world, this is the dysfunction of this worldly system.

The Torah does not offer a functional woman's posture without an authority over her. If this is the position of the Torah in the natural, why would it be different in the spirit? Y'shua said; *...bound on earth then bound in the heavenlies*[108]. Paul offered; what is natural is first then that which is spiritual.[109]

> *Note: I am not saying women do not have **any** authority but that they do not have **legal** authority to unbind a soul.*

Numbers 30:3 says;

---

[107] Please refer back to Numbers 30 in its entirety for better understanding.
[108] Matthew 18:18
[109] 1 Corinthians 15:46

> *If a woman also vow a vow unto the LORD, and bind herself by a bond...(KJV)*

Example: Lets' get back to Lucy. She went to the deliverance camp meeting without Bob to receive deliverance from a debt she vowed to pay. The debt was too much for her and had become overwhelming. It became a burden on her life and kept her bound, from functioning and flowing in the Messiah. It was a distraction to her spiritual growth.

The preacher called her up, "decrees and declares" that she is free from her bondage. Her husband did NOT declare her free from the debt. Is Lucy still bound to this debt? Yes. Lucy decrees and declares herself as free. Is Lucy still bound to this debt? Yes. Why? Let us go back to the scripture in 1 Corinthians 11 and Numbers 30. The deliverer for the woman's soul is **the man in authority to that woman**, according to the Torah.

These are the inadequacies in the deliverance ministry concerning soul bondage. The deliverance ministry's answer to the woman is to pray that Father takes away or loosens her soul from the bondage established. It is not in her authority, according to the Torah, to do so. She can only be delivered by her husband, her father if she is in her youth, in her father's house or the one who has her in bondage.

What Happened to My Authority (man)?

> *When a man vows a vow to Yahweh, or swears an oath to bind his soul with a bond, he shall not break his word; he shall do according to all that proceeds out of his mouth.*
> *Numbers 30:2 (WEB)*

Could your authority be in the hands of another man or woman? There are men who have submitted their authority, according to the Torah, by simply not posturing themselves or by not speaking up to bind or loosen a vow or oath.

Biblically, in Numbers 30:2, the Most High personally holds *men* responsible to do *all* that is vowed or put in an oath by the man. There is *not* another man who has authority over him who can cancel his vows. Another man can tell him he released him from the vow or oath, but to the Most High, you are still held bound. Men must take the responsibility for their mouths, use wisdom, and know if vows or oaths are spoken by them, they will have to give account to make it good. Meaning, be willing to do what it takes to bring dysfunction back into function, or bring injustice into righteousness.

The dangers and ramifications of this legal precedent set in the Hebrew text of Numbers 30:2 is we are offered the word "asah[110]," which is translated

---

[110] Hebrews Strong's reference # 6213

as "do." At the risk of sounding too literal and semantical, the generic verb "do" here carries a plethora of responsibilities. Here are a few.

If the man is responsible to "do," he is responsible to: commit, make, deal, offer, execute, keep, prepare, work, dress, maintain, bruise, fashion, labor, wrought, and even sin.

The point I am trying to establish is that no matter what the circumstances may be, the Most High wants a man to work until it hurts (wrought). Even when he misses the mark (sin), keeping, guarding, maintaining his word spoken (dress). Preparing for whatever attacks or adversities that may present itself. Wearing your word close to your skin (fashion), to the point of being modeled and characterized by it.

Those are just a few examples of the level of responsibility a man has when it comes to his vows and oaths. All this responsibility tied to a man's word. Ecclesiastes 5:2-3 says;

> *Don't be rash with your mouth, and don't let your heart be hasty to **utter** anything before God; for God is in heaven, and you on earth. Therefore let your words be few. For as a dream comes with a multitude of cares, so a fool's speech with a multitude of words. (WEB)*

To utter means *to offer rash words spoken outside of wisdom, usually in the form of a vow*[111]. These are the principles of our words that have been lost due to the abandonment of the Torah. When Bob was so passionate about his love for Lucy, he told her, "I'll love you forever." Is Bob still with Lucy today? Has forever come? Is Bob still bound?

Men have submitted their authority to society. Our politically correct society emasculates men from speaking up to cancel vows and oaths from those we are biblically responsible for. Society has brainwashed men and woman alike to believe women are not under the responsibility or authority of men. Dare a man have the nerve to posture himself as an authority over his wife, lest he be called a male chauvinist?

Society teaches to utter whatever comes to their heart. Society has disguised it as "free speech," which, it is speech that binds a man's soul. Remember, there is NO authority to take away these utterances for the man biblically, and men have turned the women over to societies authority, so who, what, or how is any order going to return to this lawlessness. Vows and oaths are being uttered in the hearing of men by the ones they have been put in authority over, yet how many times are men annulling the words being spoken that go against the vision they have for their family and homes?

---

[111] "Utter" -Hebrews Strong's #4008 and 981 - Ancient Hebrew Lexicon of the Bible

The authority of man is being taken by pastors. Pastors are becoming second husbands to spiritually widowed women. In what form is this happening? When a woman denies her husband as the authority over her soul and submits to a pastor-like figure in her life. If this is done in her husband's presence and he does not renounce her words, the Torah says; it shall stand as confirmed[112]. Anytime a woman vows herself to the pastor, even to the point where she claims the pastor as her covering, and the husband does not speak up against it, the husband submits his authority to the pastor. This is how pastors are becoming the second husband to spiritually widowed women. The husband can get his authority back if he would speak up for himself and take responsibility for his wife's soul.

A husband that allows a second husband causes perversion, confusion, double mindedness, infirmity, and shame in the woman. John 10:10 says,

> *The thief only comes to steal, kill, and destroy. I came that they may have life, and may have it abundantly.*

This verse is constantly used by the Christian Charismatic movement to refer to the devil, but keeping the text in context, Y'shua was referring to

---

[112] Numbers 30:7 - *And her husband heard it, and held his peace at her in the day that he heard it: then her vows shall stand, and her bonds wherewith she bound her soul shall stand. (KJV)*

the religious leaders masquerading as shepherds stealing, killing, and destroying. They are stealing wives, killing a husband's authority, and destroying their home.

Temperance

Temperance is another example of how a man can lose his authority. The Torah offers, if a man does not speak up against something he has heard, it is affirmation of agreement[113]. These neutral postures could potentially strip a man of his authority. We have already seen if a man chooses not to speak up against society, how a second authority can creep in using the form of a leader. Now we want to look at temperance.

Temperance is *your ability to show moderation and self-restraint.* Imagine Bob was a man who had a rough life, and in order to survive, he had to be street tough. In his ability to make it on the streets, he developed a temper like the Marvel comic book character *Incredible Hulk,* where he only knew two levels of temper, extremely angry or overly passive. Bob then settled down and starts a family or business to become a productive member of society. This inability to find the median for his temper means that when the situation occurs when he should be speaking up, he remains quiet. This is because he

---

[113] Numbers 30:7 - *And her husband heard it, and held his peace at her in the day that he heard it: then her vows shall stand, and her bonds wherewith she bound her soul shall stand.*

knows he can only offer a level of temperance at an extreme level. He never postures himself, yet when he does, it's fueled with rage and violence. Not being able to find the articulation and diplomacy needed to speak when needed, without anger and violence, too many settle vows goes unchecked.

Bob's attitude is; *I'm so mean and tuff that if I get involved, Ima' go off. So, you would rather my wife handle it, cause if you deal with me, you'll be sorry.*

This neutral posture keeps his family bound to a plethora of curses. His family needs a husbandman not afraid to cry, stand, establish law, and be the spiritual authority all in wisdom. The silent Bob syndrome has so many homes bound. Because he was never taught the principles and the necessity to use his words, his silence binds him and his family. Ultimately submitting his authority over to his wife.

The Disowned Child

The Torah offers us the function of how our families should be, but since we have left the principles of our forefathers, the dysfunction seems to be what we are familiar with. One of the most common dysfunctions we have seen slipping through is the dis-ownership of a child.

A blended family is defined as:

> *A family composed of a couple and their children from previous marriages.*[114]

Today, we could even broaden the definition *to a family that is comprised of a couple and their children from previous* relationships.

The blended family dynamic is not a new concept, it was also known to the ancient world of the Torah. Israel, Moshe, Y'shua, and even Paul shows us the principles of adoption[115].

It is in the areas of owning a child where we see the most dysfunction. The western concept of family requires a person to reach outside of themselves and truly take ownership of a child who is not naturally/biologically their own. While in the ancient world of the Torah, it was the righteous thing to do, and the honorable thing to do.

Western thought trains us to be about likes and dislikes, therefore, when a child is handled with that same thought process, it becomes easier to be pushed to the side. The blended family takes a commitment for the children and new parental units beyond whether they *like or dislike* each other. Hebraic concepts of love start with seeing the person as a gift first.[116] Then appreciating and honoring the gift. It would be like wanting a new computer as a gift, but

---

[114] Blended Family - Random House Unabridged dictionary 2018 first usage 1980-1985
[115] Genesis 48:16; Exodus 2:10; Matthew 1:19-20; Romans 8:14-16
[116] Love – ahav – To provide and protect what is given as privileged gift. AHL (1094) #H157 #H1890

you receive a sweater, then becoming disgruntle because of the sweater. Not until you are stranded in a winter storm, will you appreciate the sweater.

When I say take ownership of a child, I am not talking about just documentation. Ownership is more than making sure a child is provided for and all the appropriate legal paperwork is done. Ownership is truly becoming invested in the interest of the child's soul and well-being. Ownership is taking responsibility for their actions. It is *recognizing as having full claim, authority, power, dominion and possession*[117] over that child.

The turmoil caused inside a child's soul because a person who should take proper ownership, does not, is very destructive. These effects are natural and spiritual to the dynamic of a home. When a child is not *owned,* then the ability to fight, stand up, bind and loosen their soul is absent.

A father may have the desire to cancel the vows and oaths of a daughter, but if in his heart he has not owned her as land, she will discern it within herself. This will produce an unsubmitted soul. But if the father really loves her, he will be willing to fight for her. A father will need to make those verbal confessions and be willing to fight. Father's need to stand up for their daughters and be their deliverer. Even if they resist at first, be diligent because it may change her life.

---

[117] Own - Based on the Random House Unabridged Dictionary, © Random House, Inc. 2018

When a child does not have the discipline of the father added to their soul, their soul feels hated. The child may offer resistance when boundaries are attempted to be established. This is the nature of the unruly soul toward a father figure. When the lawgiver and disciplinarian is in the hands of the male, the soul can develop correct order or function. But if the child's soul recognizes you are not owning their soul, nor have taken a true vested interest, the results can be disparaging. The soul is already going to buck against order, then when you add a false since of security to it, you can only expect a confrontation.

> *One who spares the rod hates his son, But one who loves him is careful to discipline him.*
> *Proverbs 13:24 (WEB)*

Because of the political correctness bondage of society, fathers submit their ability to be the disciplinarian and lawgiver of the home. In my experience, I have come across children who have felt their father doesn't love them because he refuses to discipline them. There is a consciousness of order that seems to be in the soul.[118]

David, before he was commissioned to be King of Israel, had a father who didn't even include him in the count of his sons. Samuel came to his home to appoint a king by examining all of Jesse's sons, yet

---

[118] Conscience bearing witness – Romans 2:15

David was not called to attend until after all the *jocks* were rejected. What value did his father have for him when he was not even considered to be called in from work to fellowship?

> *Jesse made seven of his sons to pass before Samuel. Samuel said to Jesse, Yahweh has not chosen these. Samuel said to Jesse, Are here all your children? He said, There remains yet the youngest, and, behold, he is keeping the sheep. Samuel said to Jesse, Send and get him; for we will not sit down until he come here. He sent, and brought him in. Now he was ruddy, and withal of a beautiful face, and goodly to look on. Yahweh said, Arise, anoint him; for this is he.*
> *1 Samuel 16:10-12 (WEB)*

Just consider all the different ways a child's soul could be bound just because someone was not willing to step up and own them. There is going to be a fight for ownership, but they need to see you're willing to put in the effort for them.

> *Note: I am not talking about abandonment, I am talking about never owning them in the first place. Seeing the gift as a curse and not as the blessing the Father has ordained them to be.*

Eight

FROM INFIRMITY TO FREEDOM

Proverbs tells us the key to overcome infirmity is the same solution that Paul offers in Romans chapter 8. When infirmity is present, firmness is needed. Proverbs says;

> *Through wisdom is a house builded; and by understanding it is established: And by knowledge shall the chambers be filled with all precious and pleasant riches.* ***A wise man is strong; yea, a man of knowledge increaseth strength.*** *For by wise counsel thou shalt make thy war: and in multitude of*

> *counsellors there is safety.*
> *Proverbs 24:3-6 (KJV)*

This Proverb has more than what I am able to discuss currently, but let's pull out this phrase; *"knowledge increasth strength."* The word *strength* in Hebrew is Koach. Koach carries the meaning; *to be firm, wealthy, and fruitful,* amongst other meanings.[119] In order to increase in firmness, there needs to be knowledge applied.

The Anointing Destroys the Yoke.[120]

When someone is bound in a state of infirmity, the Torah has a law to help them after their time in infirmity is fulfilled. But the weakness of the law is when the time has been fulfilled, yet the cycle is not broken. When the cycle seems to carry on from one season to the next without a transition. The law has a remedy for the status change, but the weakness of the law is man's need to apply it. This is where the intimacy with Y'shua is necessary. If a soul is already perverted and infirm, then it would be like a depressed person trying to find the motivation to read a book on how not to be depressed.

The scriptures offer that there is a level of intimacy with the Messiah that is needed to come to a

---

[119] Strength -Koach Hebrew Strong's #H3581
[120] Isaiah 10:27

place of firmness.[121] It is only through the intimate relationship with the Messiah Y'shua that this firmness can be accomplished.

The commonly known word in Hebrew used for *knowledge* is Da'ath, but at its root is the word Yadah. I prefer to point people to the Yadah because it represents the picture of a man that works for the opportunity of intimacy.[122] Like a man that would court a woman, Yadah is a picture of that kind of knowledge. The type of knowledge found in Genesis 4:1 when Adam *knew* his wife Eve. Once again, this knowledge is not information, but intimacy through work.

Are you determined? How serious are you about being free? Work is necessary for fruit and increase. Power is necessary to get through the season of infirmity, iniquity, and bondage. In order to produce fruit, then have seed and a chance to sow that seed, we are going to need to truly work.

Hebrew; there is nothing in the Torah that offers a change in appetite, only the knowledge of the unclean appetite. The reason why you will not find this in the Torah is because *the Torah is the knowledge of sin*.[123] Subsequently then, the work of the law is not the *work* needed to be applied.

Christian; you can go to a Benny Hinn conference and get healed and still return to the products that got you into your bondage in the first

---

[121] Proverbs 24:5; Matthew 7:22-23; 2 Timothy 2:19
[122] AHL – Knowledge 1085 Yadah - #H3045; #H3046
[123] Knowledge of sin – Romans 3:20

place. So, chasing quick fixes is not the *work* necessary to come to a place of firmness and deliverance.

Throughout this first edition, I have offered a few solutions to the most common areas of soul bondage that is experienced. My goal, though, is not to just show the keys to freedom, but to also put the demand on each reader to go and to set someone else free.

> *The Spirit of the Lord GOD is upon me; because the LORD hath anointed me to preach good tidings unto the meek; he hath sent me to bind up the brokenhearted, to proclaim liberty to the captives, and the opening of the prison to them that are bound; To proclaim the acceptable year of the LORD, and the day of vengeance of our God; to comfort all that mourn;*
> *Isaiah 61:1-2 (KJV)*

One of the biggest deceptions that is sold to the perfectly capable individuals is that the call to be a deliverer is for leaders, pastors, or some specially gifted individual. This cannot be further from the truth. The Spirit of the Master YHWH is on *you;* because YHWH has anointed *you.*

Isaiah is very specific in the text. The anointing that the Most High has given you is to be used for His *work.* Proclaiming liberty to the captives and releasing those who are bound. The anointing completely capable of breaking your yoke and the yoke of others.

Building the precept in Isaiah with the precept in Proverbs, we can better understand the assignment on each one of our lives. Press in toward the relationship with Y'shua, work for an intimate relationship with him. When we do that, in return, we gain the firmness needed to be set free and the anointing needed to set others free.

Study the stories of Y'shua in the gospels. People were healed and delivered, then driven to spread the goodness of their deliverance to others. I am talking about the same thing. But I want to go even further. In our pursuit of Y'shua and the intimacy with him, I understand that we are going to begin to look less like ourselves.

We are taking on the task of setting our loved ones free as we face HaSatan's imps head on. Only through fortitude, which comes from our confidence in our relationship with Him, will we be able to stand. The closer we develop our relationship with Him, the more we will learn about our own anointing he has placed in us.

The anointing that he has placed in each one of us is not by happenstance but has been placed there with a purpose. Incubating with the purpose to hatch, not rot.

The more intimate a soul is with Y'shua, the more Y'shua is seen in the life of the person. As the symbiotic relationship develops, the *knowledge* of His anointing in us becomes more pronounced.

When we begin to know our anointing, we will then be able to know our strength. When we are intimately in tune with the source of our anointing, we are then empowered with the confidence, the firmness, and power to be effective in His Kingdom's movement on the earth.

I encourage every one of you to be strong in the Messiah, speak up, stand up, rise up, and grab someone else to escape with you toward freedom.

When you know your anointing, you know your strength. When you know the source of your power, the person Y'shua HaMashiach, you know your strength. You are then no longer weak but strong, no longer bound but free.
-Hoshea

ABOUT HOSHEA

Hoshea was born Gerald M. Williams Jr. and raised in the service of YHWH to Bishop Gerald Williams Sr. and Diane Williams. Being full of the anointing of his grandfather Bishop Charlie M. Davis and his parents, Hoshea decided to live completely for the Messiah in 1999.

Since his dedication to YHWH, he had multiple mentors come into his life teaching and training him in the word, the gifts of the Spirit, and leadership. Hoshea is now a bondservant of Y'shua HaMashiach, ordained by the Spirit of our Living Elohim, and ordained by man for men (least the gospel needs any man's approval to be preached) by Pastor Rabbi Ralph Messer of Simchat Torah Beit Midrash of Denver, Colorado under the direction of his father and eldership. He is now the community leader of a group of Messianic Hebrews in Columbus, Ohio under the name of The House of Israel Ohio LLC.

The Call:

Raised in the Non-Denominational Christian Charismatic movement, Hoshea began to be used supernaturally by the Spirit at the tender age of 6 when he began to play drums during praise and worship at his father's congregation. With no previous experience of playing, he recalls telling his mom when asked; What made you start playing? The young, six-year-old Hoshea replied; "God told me to."

Faithfully continuing in the faith as a teenager and young adult, Hoshea started to be faced with the temptations of life. This time of his life gave him the powerful testimony of transformation. Once filled with the Set-apart Spirit, he immediately felt the demand of ministry in his heart.

Father has called Hoshea to reach the nations with the Gospel of conversion and deliverance. In 2007, at the beginning of the new Jewish civil New Year, the Messiah Y'shua imparted a word to him that "he hasn't seen anything yet. The level of which The Most High can reach HIS potential is us; we haven't even begun to scratch the surface." This word resonated in his heart the entire year. Hoshea continues to see Elohim consistently show how much more He has for those who keep His commands, seek after His face, and follow His instructions.

With the support of his beautiful wife and family of three kids, Hoshea aspires to be the voice for the hurting communities. Bringing the knowledge of the rights a believer in the Messiah has, through his

Kingdom of provision and blessings, accessed by a lifestyle of obedience to Y'shua's voice.

Accomplishments:

His accomplishments include: Two movies: "Slavery in the Torah" and Death to Life; Multiple CD series, such as; Providence and Adversity; to local work in his community, including youth empowerment studies, praise and worship team leader, congregational leader, mentor, evangelist, teacher, outreach ministries (local and international), father, husband, entrepreneur, and councilor.

His maturation process has given him the ability to understand the necessary keys needed for soul deliverance. The application of these keys has allowed deliverance to come to families in areas of their lives, such as: Family function, clarity of hearing to the voice of His Spirit, financial stability, courage in men, cures from generational diseases (both soul and physical), to name just a few.

Areas of Study:

Hoshea has equipped himself well with knowledge in Divinity, Hebrew Roots, Ancient Hebrew word meanings, Messianic One House, Messianic Two House, Christian History, Christian Theory, Mishnah (writings of Rambam), the Talmud, Hebrew Israelite doctrines, and an assortment of diverse views that he has or has not been taken into consideration. "The best witness and credential that I have is the Spirit of the Messiah, and the manifestation of His spiritual fruit through me," says Hoshea.

My Personal Soul Bondage:

Starting in the fourth and fifth grade, my soul was exposed to voyeurism. By the time I was in the seventh grade, I had a hardcore porn collection of five movies. My wife tells me how she was never even exposed to pornography till I bought it around to her before and after we were married. Ministering with the monkey of lust on my back made me began to search. The infirmity in my walk that I experienced was not only frustrating, but embarrassing. I recognized there was something missing in my walk with the Messiah, so everyone told me I needed the Spirit. I received the Spirit, then I was told I needed to get the fire of the spirit, the worship of the spirit, the joy of the spirit, the power of the spirit, and so I became a prayer warrior. So many answers, but I was never offered principles that caused me to take ownership of my iniquity and speak out against the corruption in my soul. This has caused me to have a heart for those in the broken system of medicating problems and not getting to the root cause. The principles that I speak of are from the law, and most evangelicals are so scared of falling into the bondage of legalism that they would rather stay bound to sin.

REFERENCES

Torah – Teaching and instructions of the Most High God, the five books of Moses, often mistranslated as law, #H8451 & #H3384

Y'shua – Name of the Messiah in the NT meaning "Salvation". Translated at times as Jesus, Yeshua, Yahshua, Yahawashi even Yehoshua

Elohim – Literally meaning Mighty One or Powers whether the supreme power or celestial powers

HaSatan – the adversary - often translated as Satan

Exegesis – critical explanation or interpretation of a text or portion of a text, especially of the Bible

Sin – Hebrew word Chattah meaning; to miss the mark. The mark being His teaching and instructions

Iniquity – Hebrew word Avon H5771 – perversity, crooked, moral evil, transgression passed on generationally

The Most High – Often referred to as the Most High God, Elohim the power. These is a universal, generic term. Commonly translated as God and LORD. Also interchangeable with YHWH, Yah, YahoWah, Yahuah, Yahweh, Yehowah and on.

Oath – To yoke a binding agreement including the curse for violating the oath. Hebrews Strong's # 7621 and 423

Vow - Promises to perform an act if another performs a certain act. Hebrews Strong's #H2385

Chattah #H2401 – An offense. Error -AHL #H2402 #H2403 - An act or condition of ignorant or imprudent deviation from a code of behavior. A missing of the target in the sense of making a mistake

Transgression #H6586 – Rebellion. To sin with an high hand. Intentional sin.

Wisdom – Is your ability to discern difference, specifically the difference between right and wrong. Then Deuteronomy 4:6 says the Torah "is your wisdom and your understanding in the sight of the nations"

Grace – (traditional definition) an allowance of time after a debt or bill has become payable granted to the debtor before suit can be brought against him or her or a penalty applied:

(Christian definition) Unmerited favor. Salvation and forgiveness through Jesus Christ that is not deserved and withholding the judgment that is deserved.

(Hebraic definition) Empowerment to keep His Torah via His spirit

YHWH – tetragrammaton for the sacred name of The Most High God. The one that exist. YahWeh, Yahuah, Yehowah, Yahovah etc.

Soul – #H5315 nephesh

Dualism - The conjunction of two (usually opposing) entities or principles.

Trinitarianism – Belief in the trinity by which God is considered as existing in three persons.

Wicked - An action that causes a stain of immorality. H#5765, #5766, #5767

Ruach HaKodesh – Set-Apart Spirt often translated as Holy Spirit and Holy Ghost

Blakemore, Colin and Jennett, Sheila. *The Oxford Companion to the Body*. Oxford University Press 2001

World Encyclopedia 2005, originally published by Oxford University Press 2005

Webster's New Millennium Dictionary of English, Preview Edition (v 0.9.7). June 2008

James Orr, M.A., D.D., General Editor. *International Standard Bible Encyclopedia* Published in 1915, 1939; public domain.

Wigoder, Geoffrey *Encyclopedia of Judaism* 1989 The Jerusalem Publishing House, Ltd. edition

Harris, Stephen L. *Understanding the Bible* 1937 – 7th edition McGraw -Hill Copyright © 2007

Bouvier, John. *A Law Dictionary*, Published 1856.

Black's Law Dictionary Free 2nd Ed. and The Law Dictionary

Random House Dictionary, © Random House, Inc

Dictionary.com Unabridged. Random House, Inc. 09 Jun. 2016

The Concise Oxford Dictionary of World Religions 1997

McKim, Donald. *The Westminster Dictionary of Theological Terms* second edition © 2014

Smith, Dr. William. *Smith's Bible Dictionary*. Published in 1863; public domain

Strong, James. *Strong's Exhaustive Concordance* by, S.T.D., LL.D. Published in 1890; public domain

Benner, Jeff A. *Ancient Hebrew Lexicon of the Bible*. Copyright © 2006Ancient Hebrew Research Center ISBN: 1589397762

American Tract Society Dictionary of the Holy Bible

M.G. Easton M.A., D.D. *Easton's Bible Dictionary* third edition. Published in 1897; public domain

King James Version of the Holy Bible (KJV) (also known as the Authorized Version). Published in 1769; public domain

The World English Bible (WEB) is a Public Domain (no copyright) Modern English translation of the Holy Bible. 1901

URGENT PLEA!

Thank You For Reading My Book!

I really appreciate all of your feedback, and I love hearing what you have to say.

I need your input to make the next version of this book and my future books even better.

Please leave me a helpful review on Amazon letting me know what you thought of the book.

For speaking engagements, workshops, classes and bookings. Contact Hoshea at: soulbondage.com – admin@houseofisraelohio.com - 6146001377

Thank you so much!
~ Gerald "Hoshea" Williams Jr.

Made in the USA
Columbia, SC
20 June 2019